SHATTERED PSYCHE

2nd Ed., Vol 1(3)

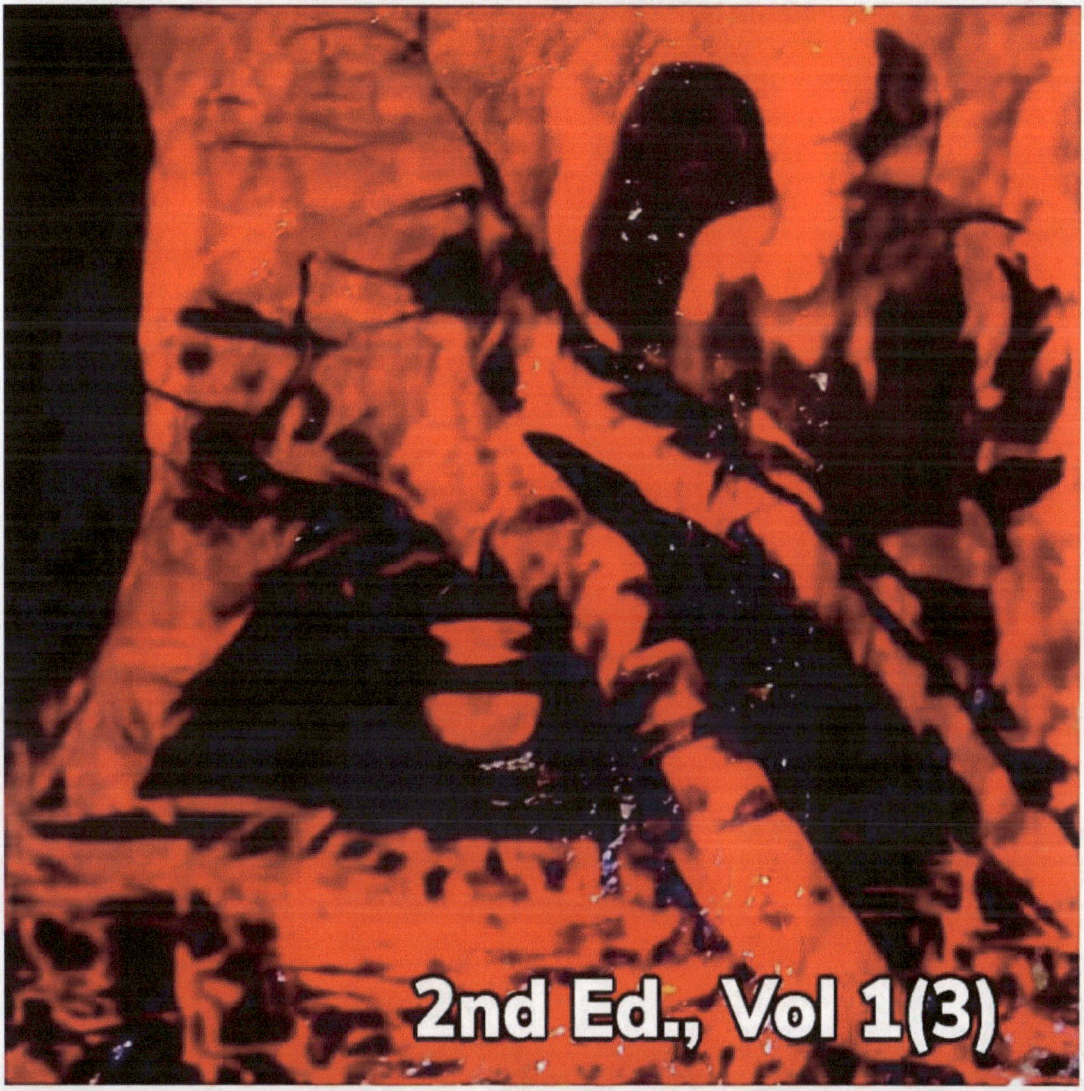

I Ain't Your Marionette

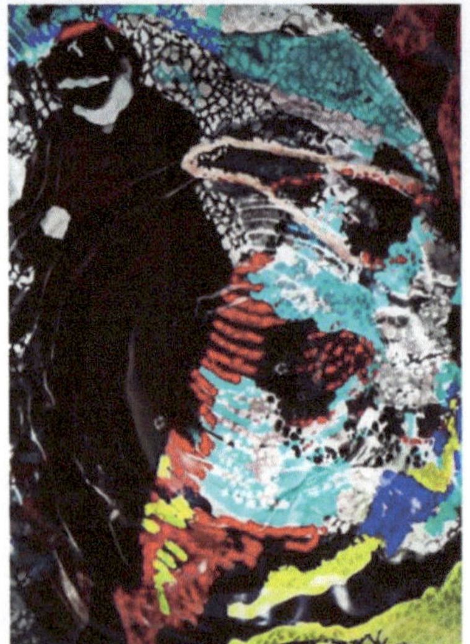

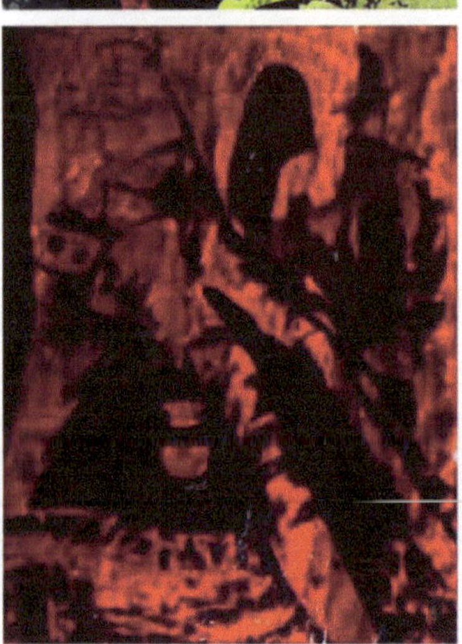

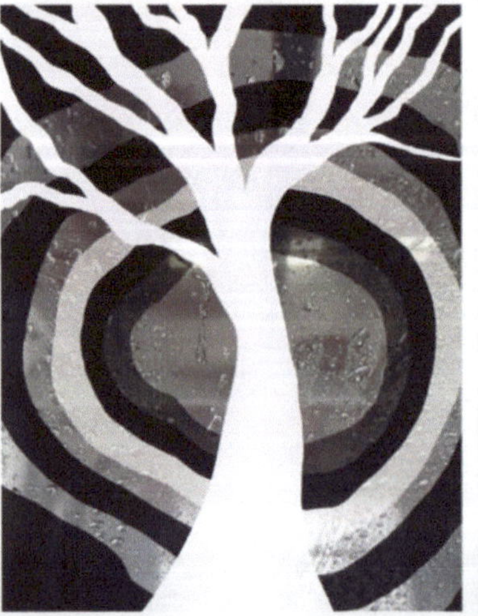

What People are saying about Shattered Psyche 2nd Ed. Vol 1(3)…

Incredible work, each artist pours their soul into each piece. You can feel the intent behind each color or shade chosen. Some amazing work. I look forward to this group's next collaboration as well as their independent works.

~~ Corey Jones

Kintsugi is the Japanese art of mending broken things by piecing them back together, filling the cracks with gold. This process allows for something thought to be broken to in fact be transformed into something new. This artistic expression celebrates the flaws and imperfections and some maybe even argue, improves upon what once was. The Shattered Psyche Anthology is a wonderful expression of the Kintsugi concept. The artists take the broken and shattered pieces of their psyche and mend them beautifully back together in art form. Metaphorically lacing the world within their mind together with the tangible world of art right in front of the viewer. The artists allegorically mold what's shattered into something whole and exciting. The art here is striking and stunning and the book is with its weight in gold.

~~ Joe Mykut,
author of Beautiful Boy

"Oochinaywin" in Ojibwe Saulteaux means acquiring a self inflicted spiritual injury that turns into physical disease.

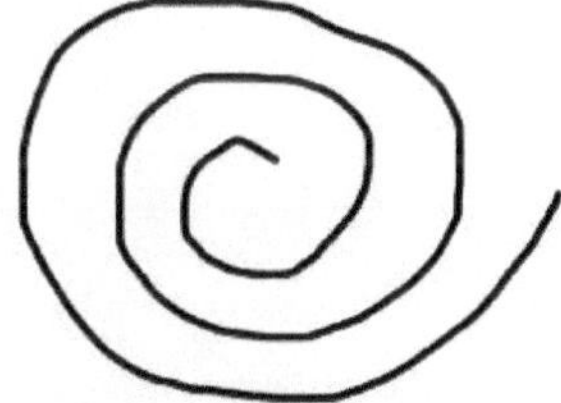

Healing the soul, heals the body.

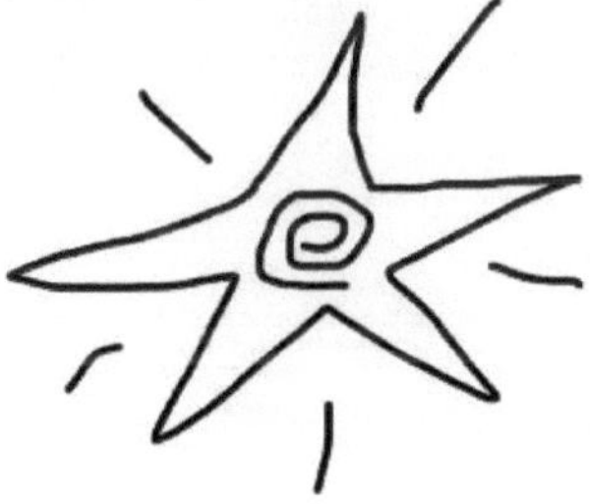

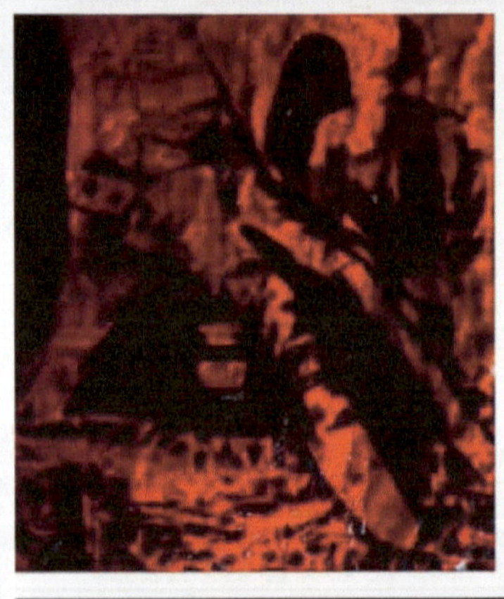
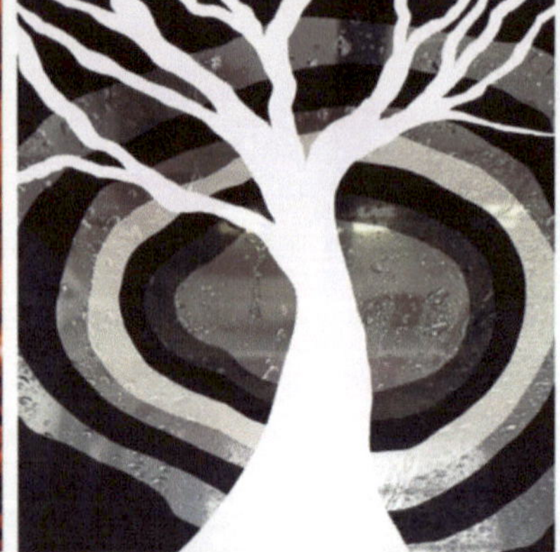
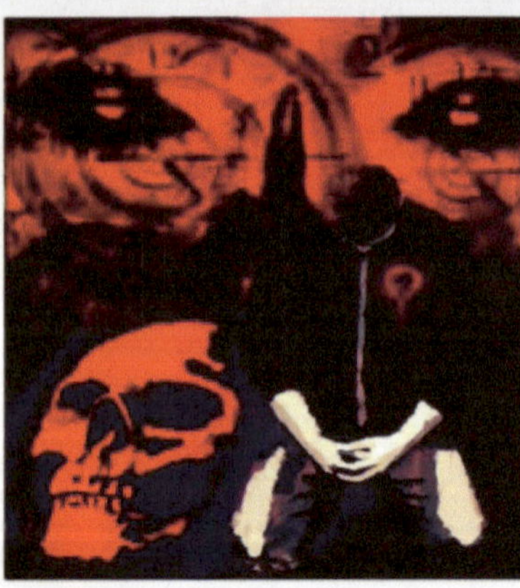
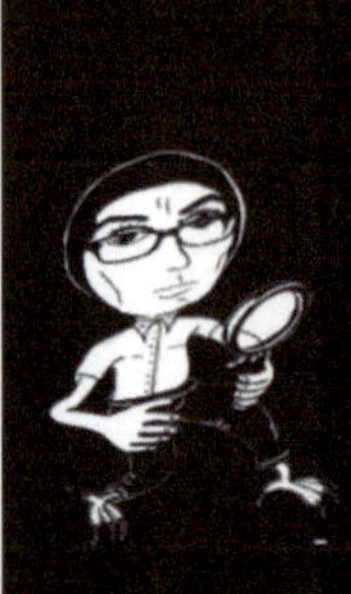

DEDICATED TO ALL POSSESSED BY THE SPIRIT OF CREATION

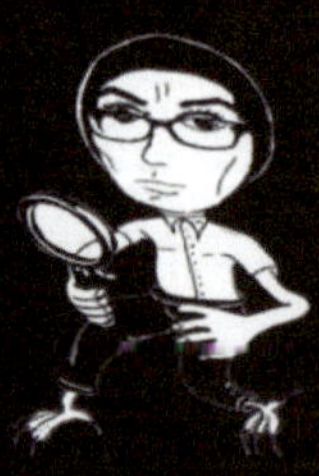
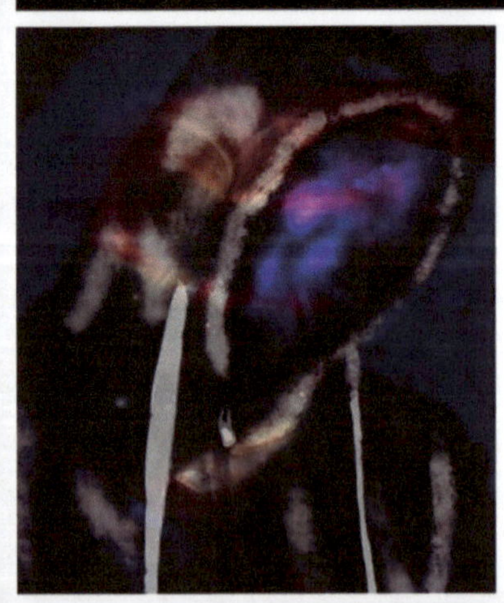
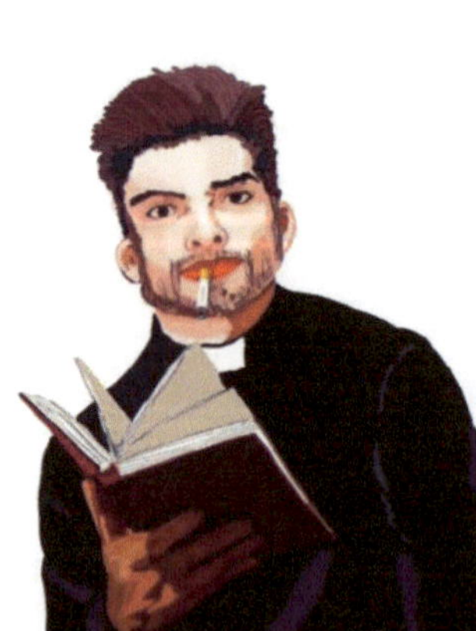
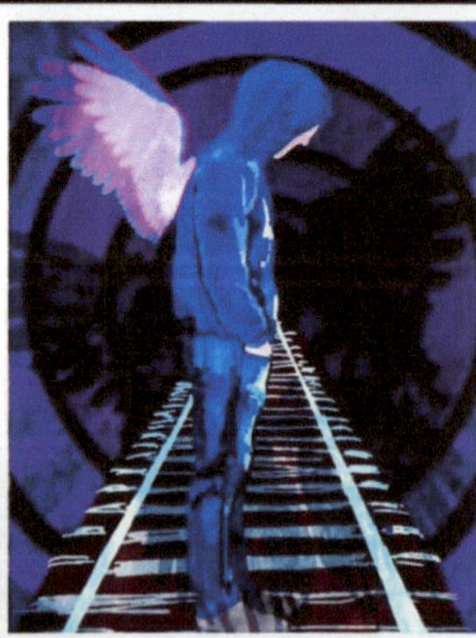

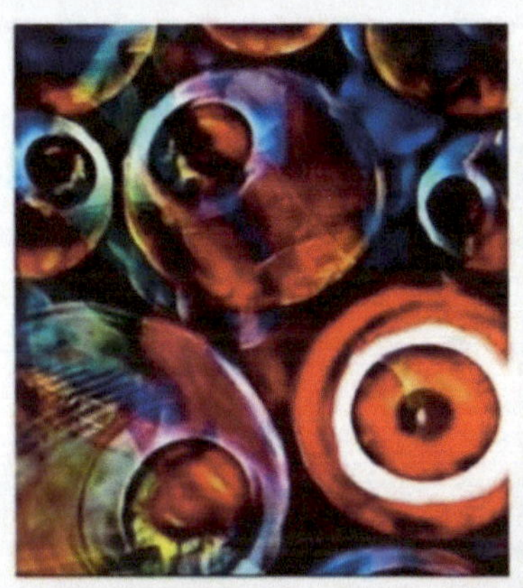
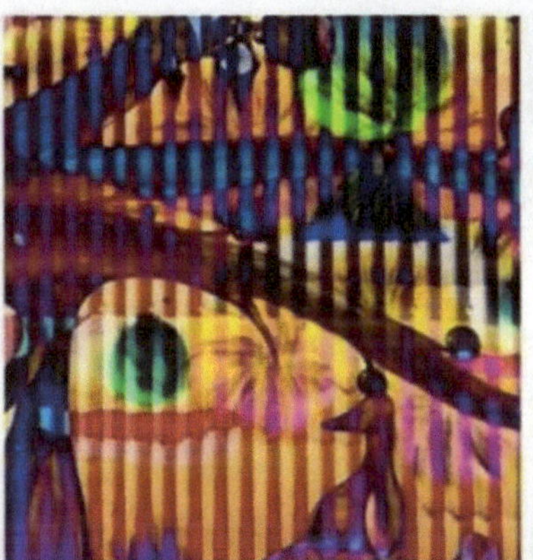
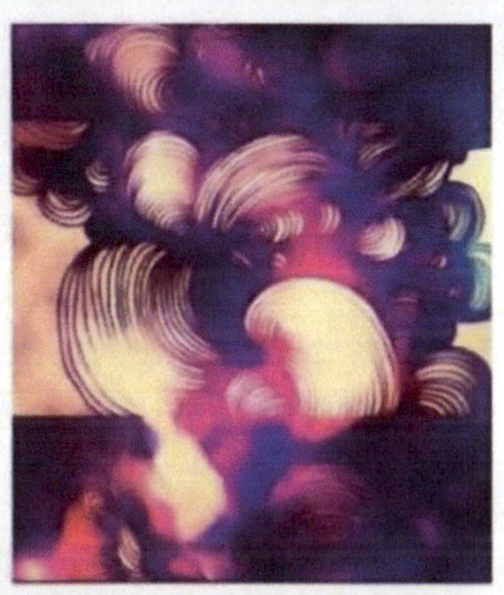

About the Collection:

An eye-popping collection of art filled with beauty and emotion from 6 women who have rebuilt their lives and grown strength and creativity from their struggles.

– Alycia Hodge

(Author / Artist / Editor)

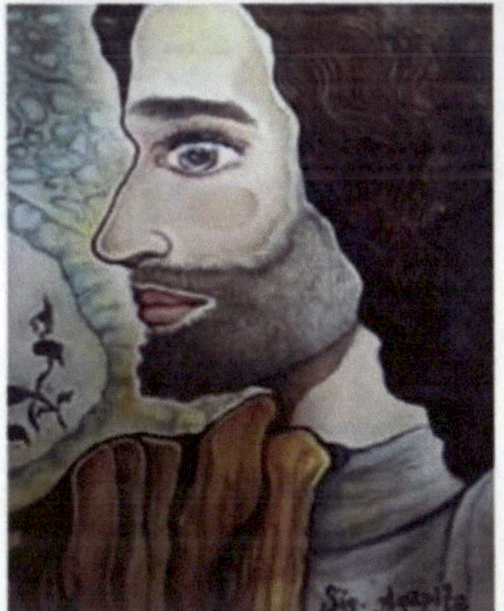
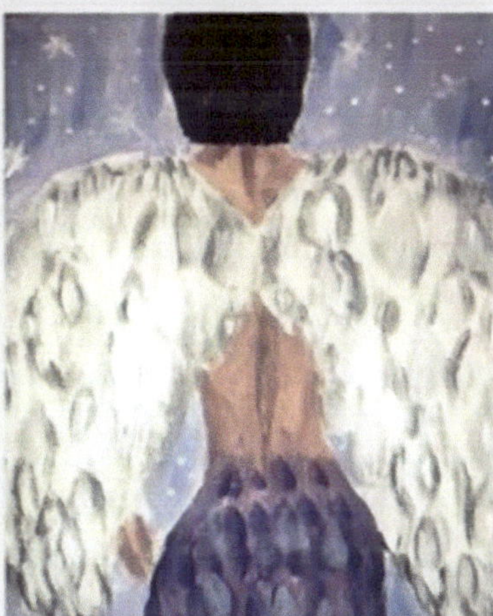
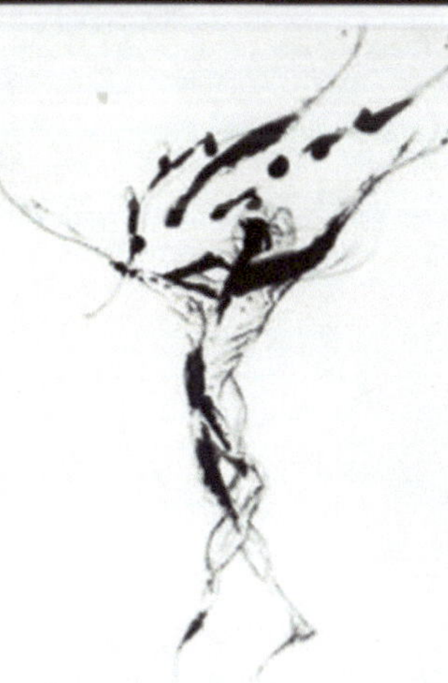

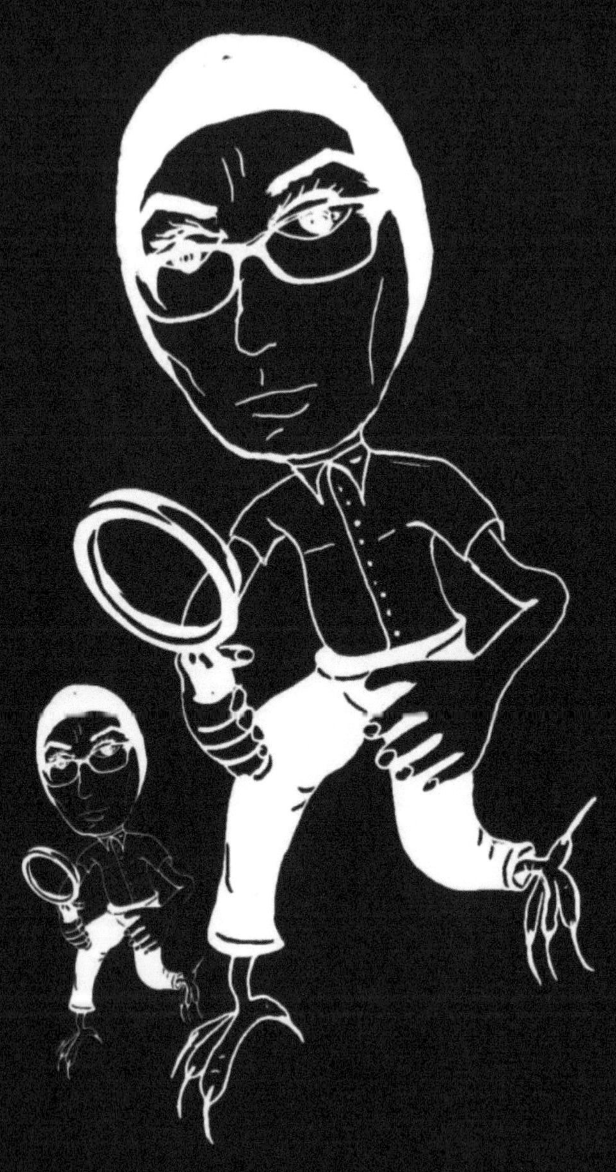

TABLE OF CONTENTS

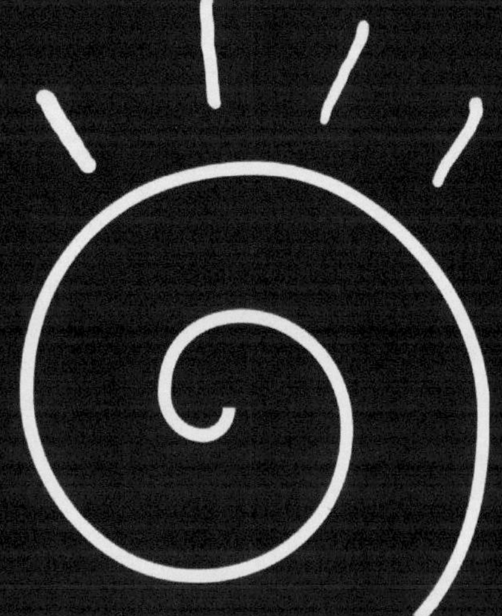

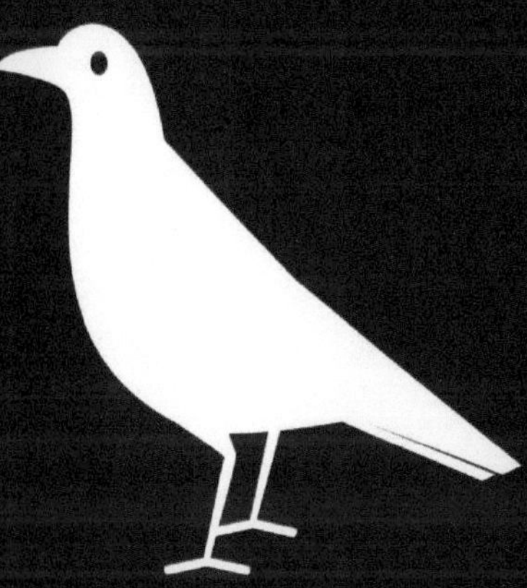

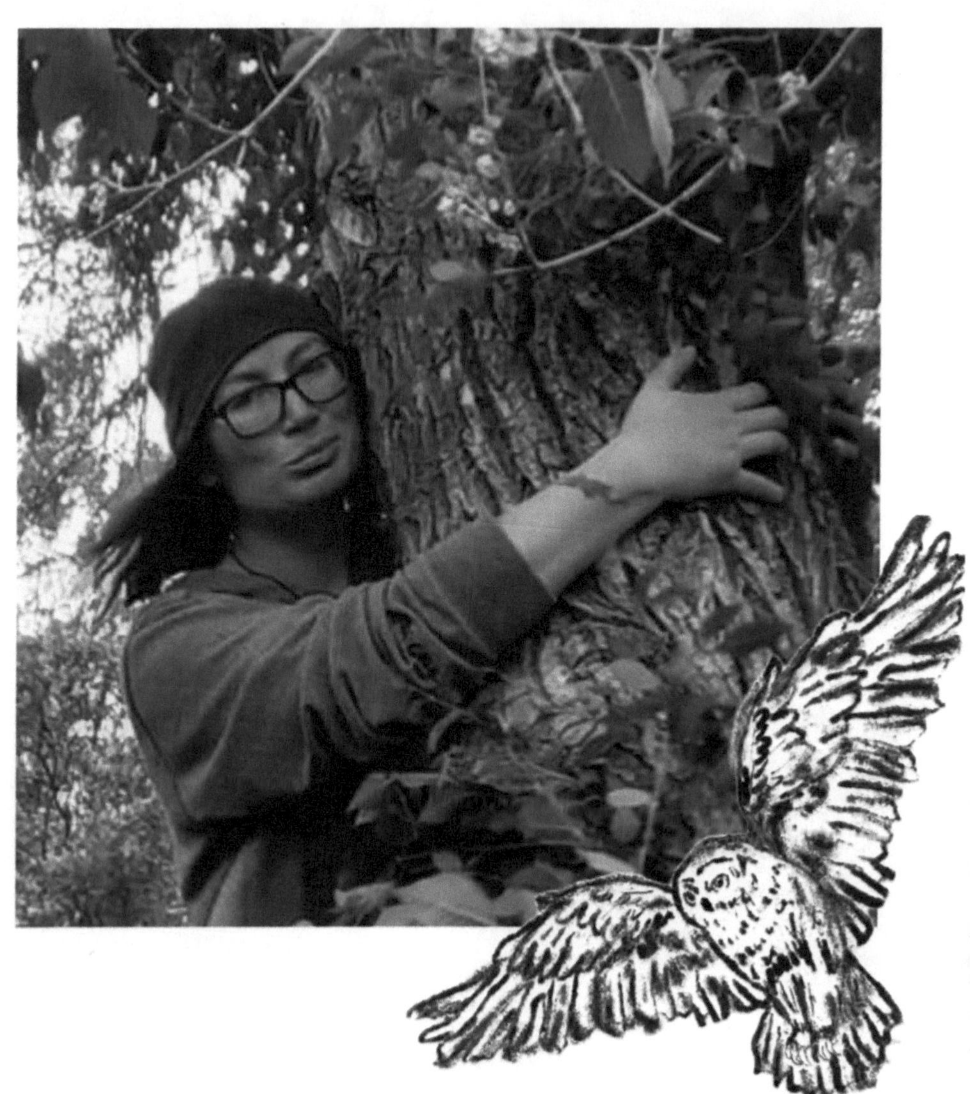

Marie Moldovan

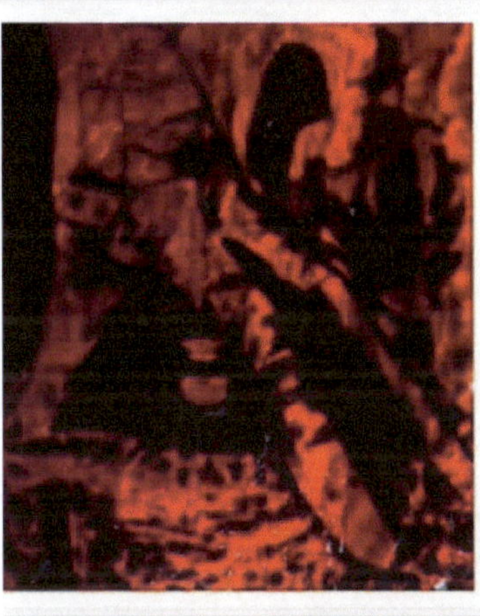

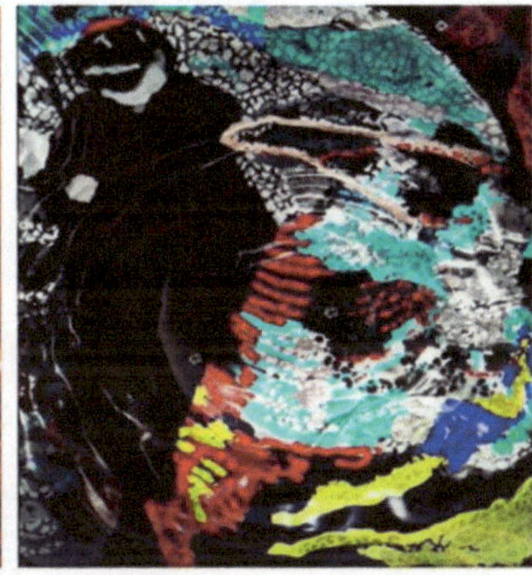

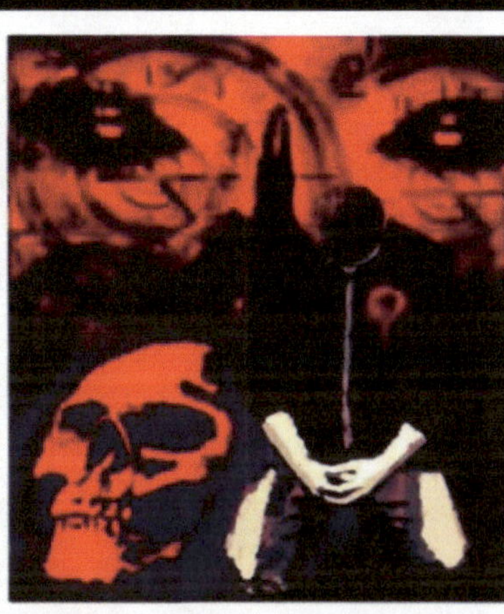

About Marie Moldovan

MARIE MOLDOVAN IS A SASKATCHEWAN NATIVE AND ONTARIO IMMIGRANT WHO BELIEVES ART TO BE EXPRESSION OF ESSENCE. S/HE ALWAYS LOVED TO CREATE, BUT DIDN'T REALIZE S/HE HAD ANY TALENT UNTIL HE/R ELEMENTARY TEACHER MR. BRAUN COMMISSIONED HER TO DO CLASS CARICATURES. CURRENTLY, MARIE USES ART TO EXPRESS THAT WHICH S/HE CANNOT VERBALIZE.

MORE ABOUT MARIE CAN BE FOUND AT:
HTTPS://RUSTYSDIGITALART.COM

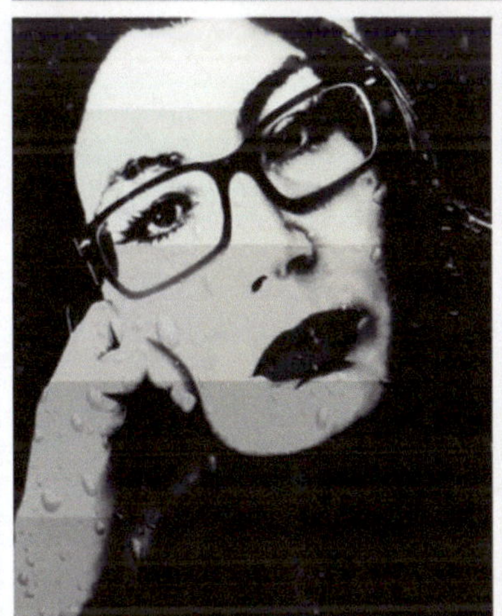

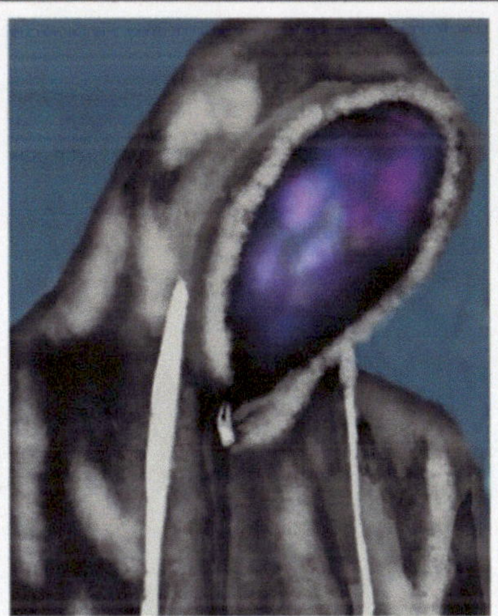

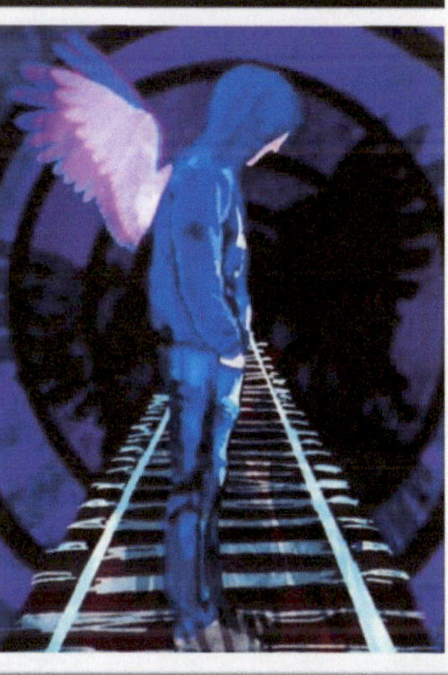

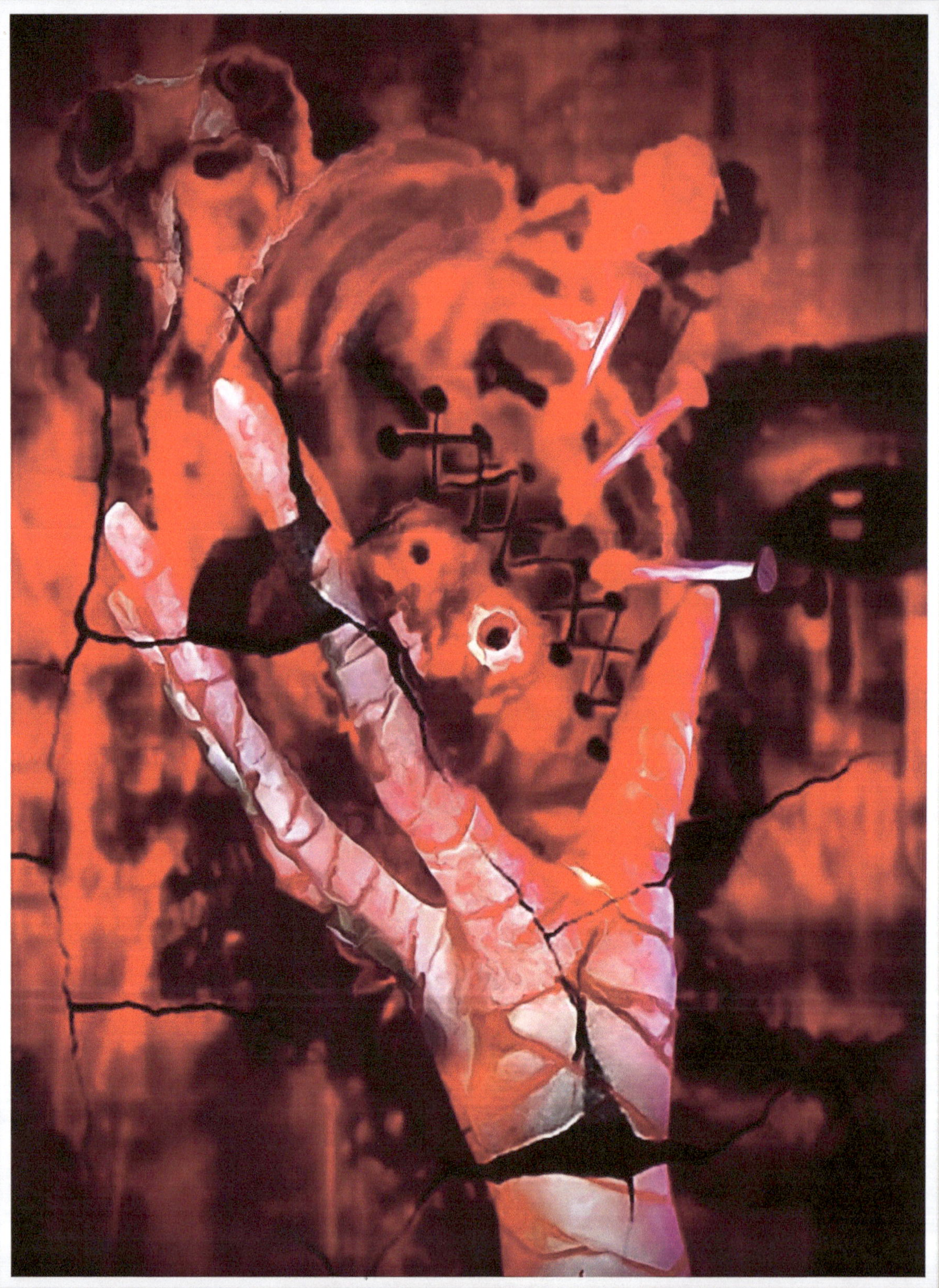

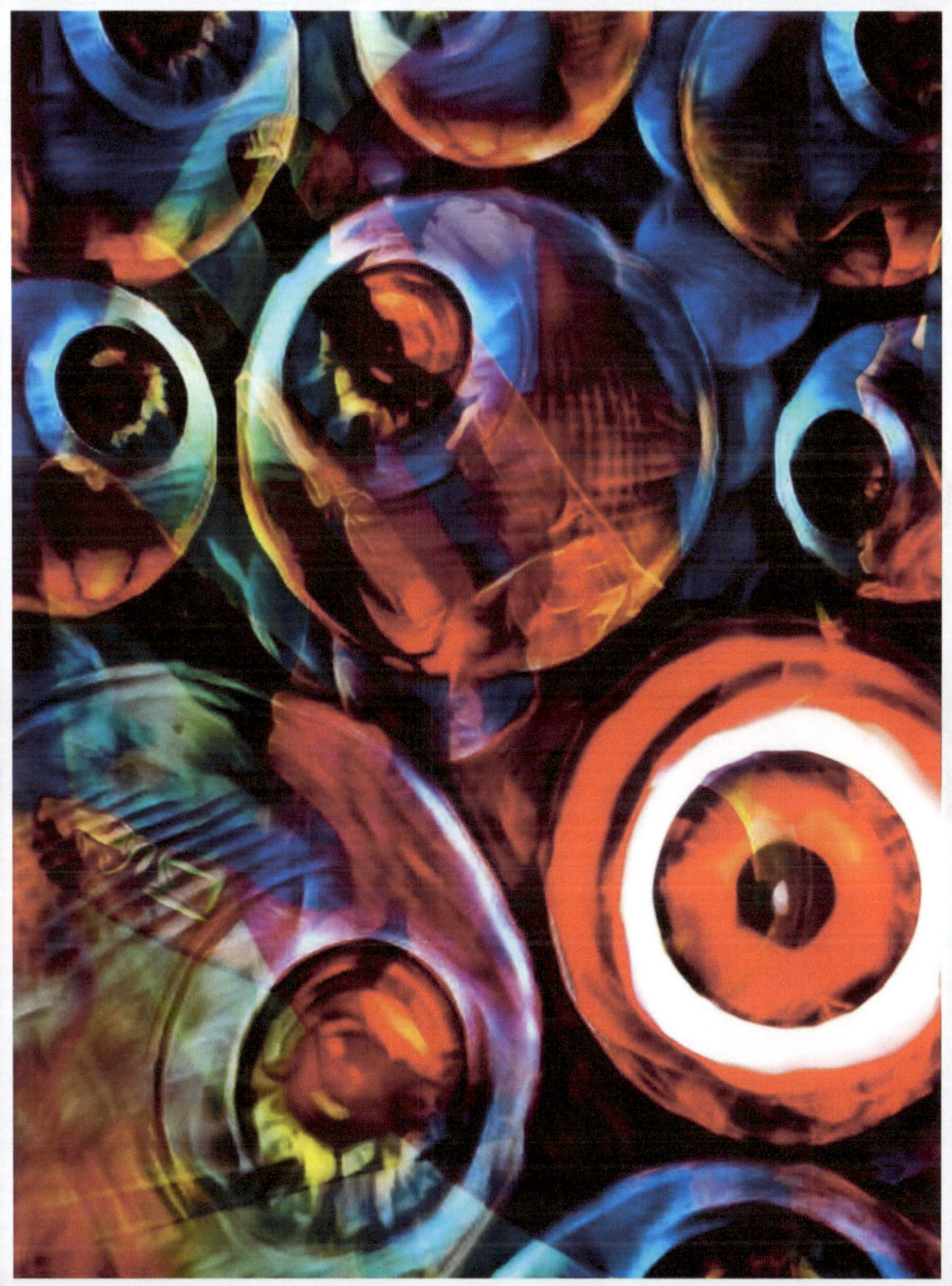

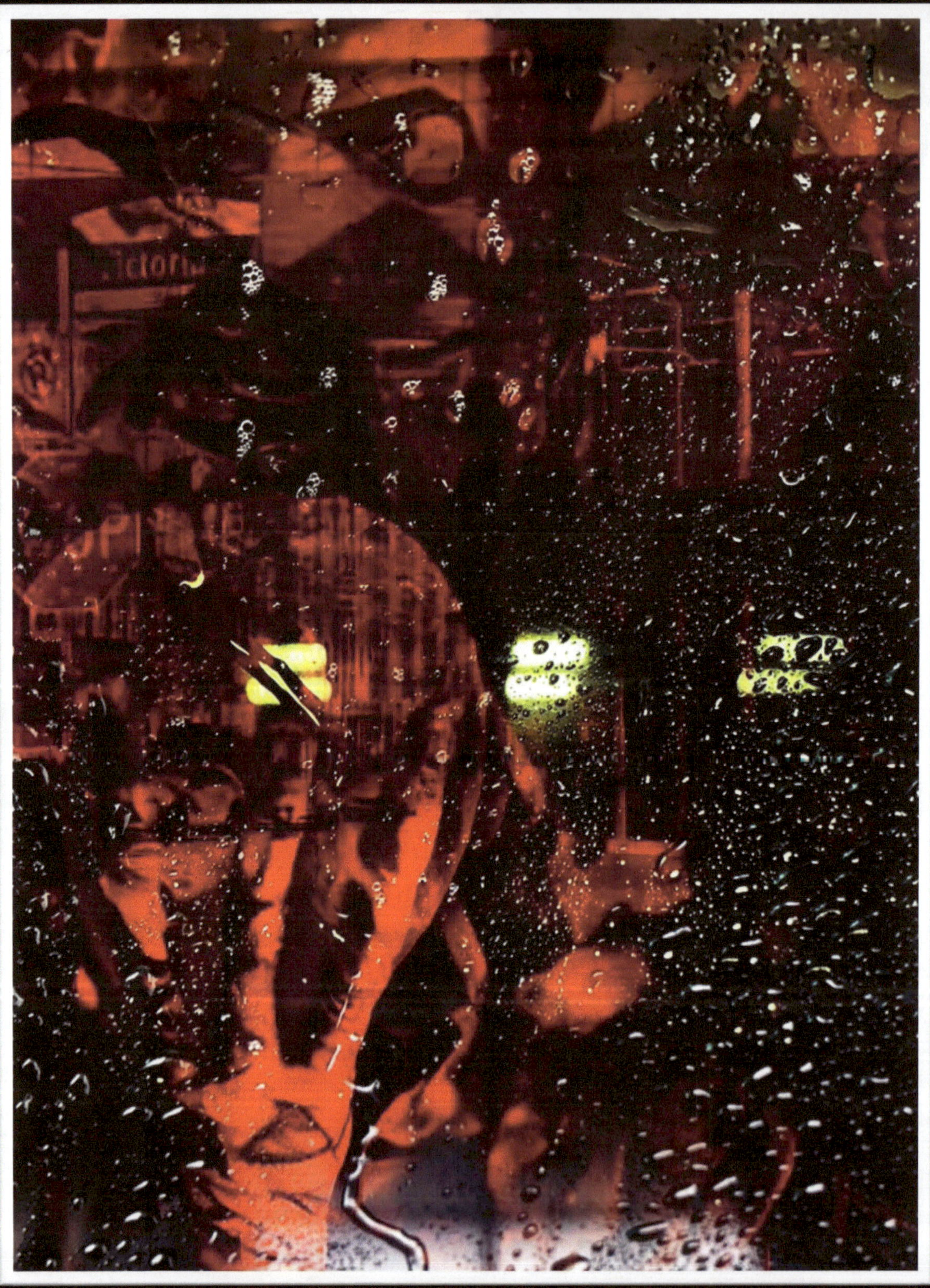

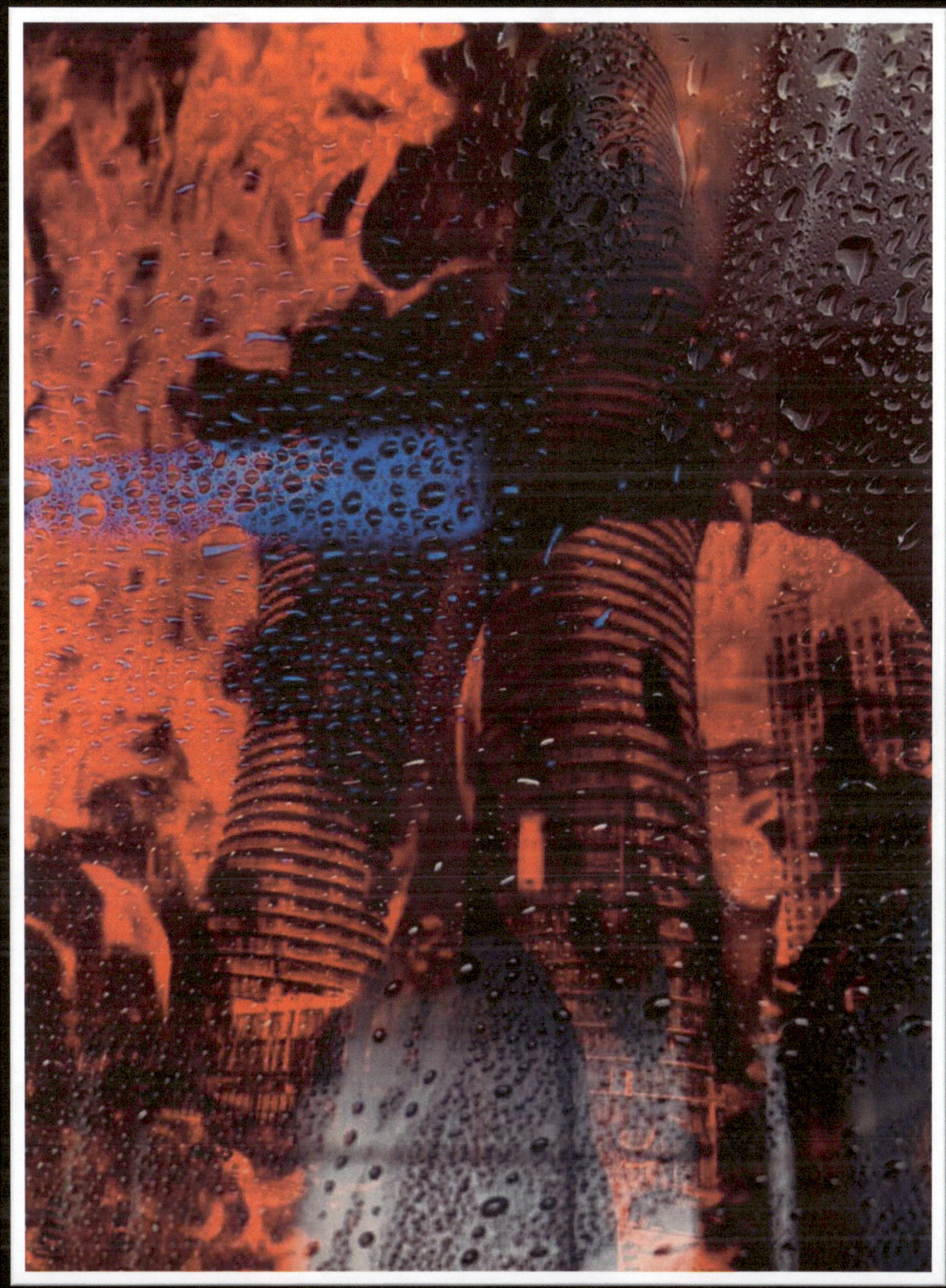

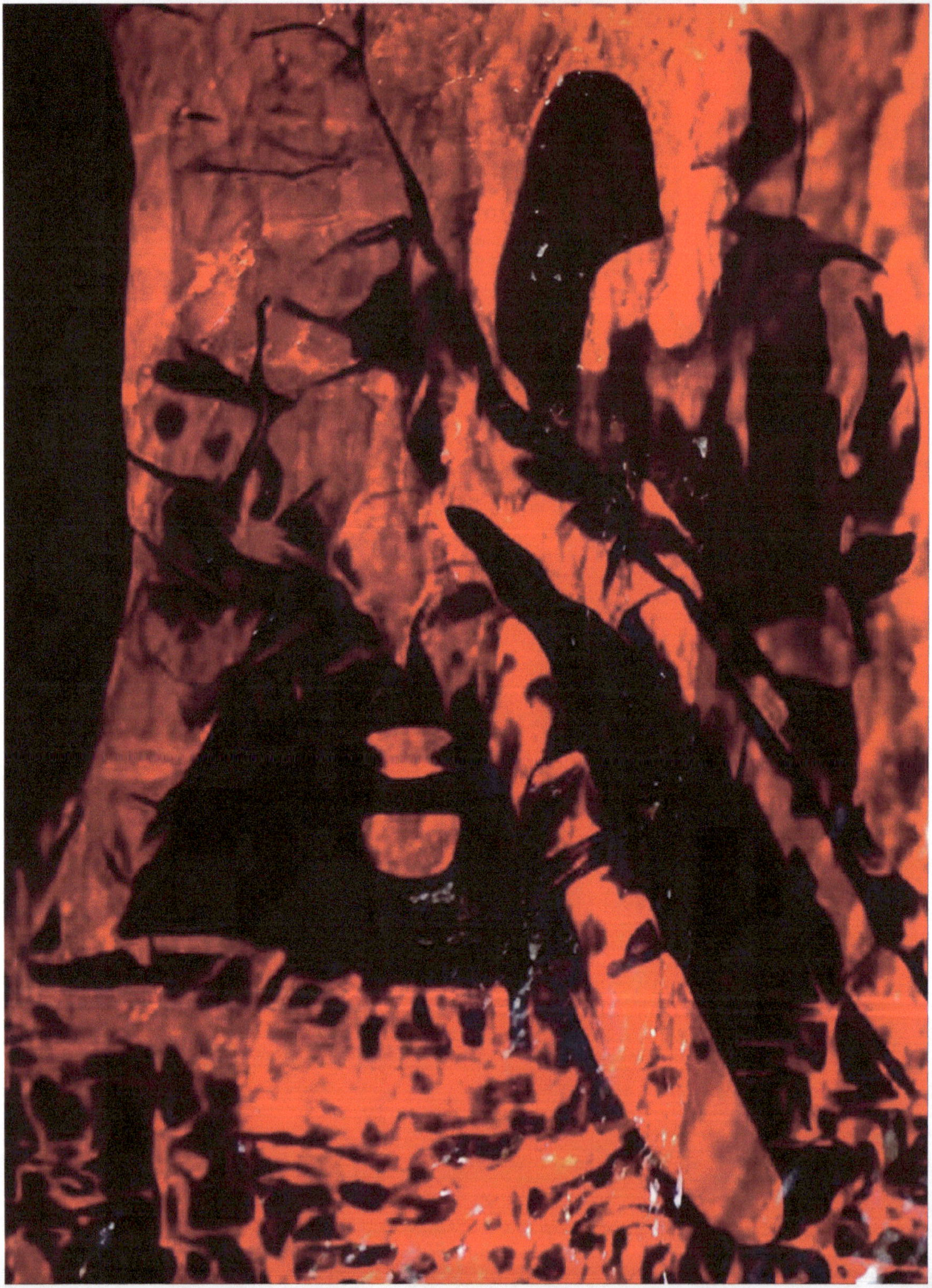

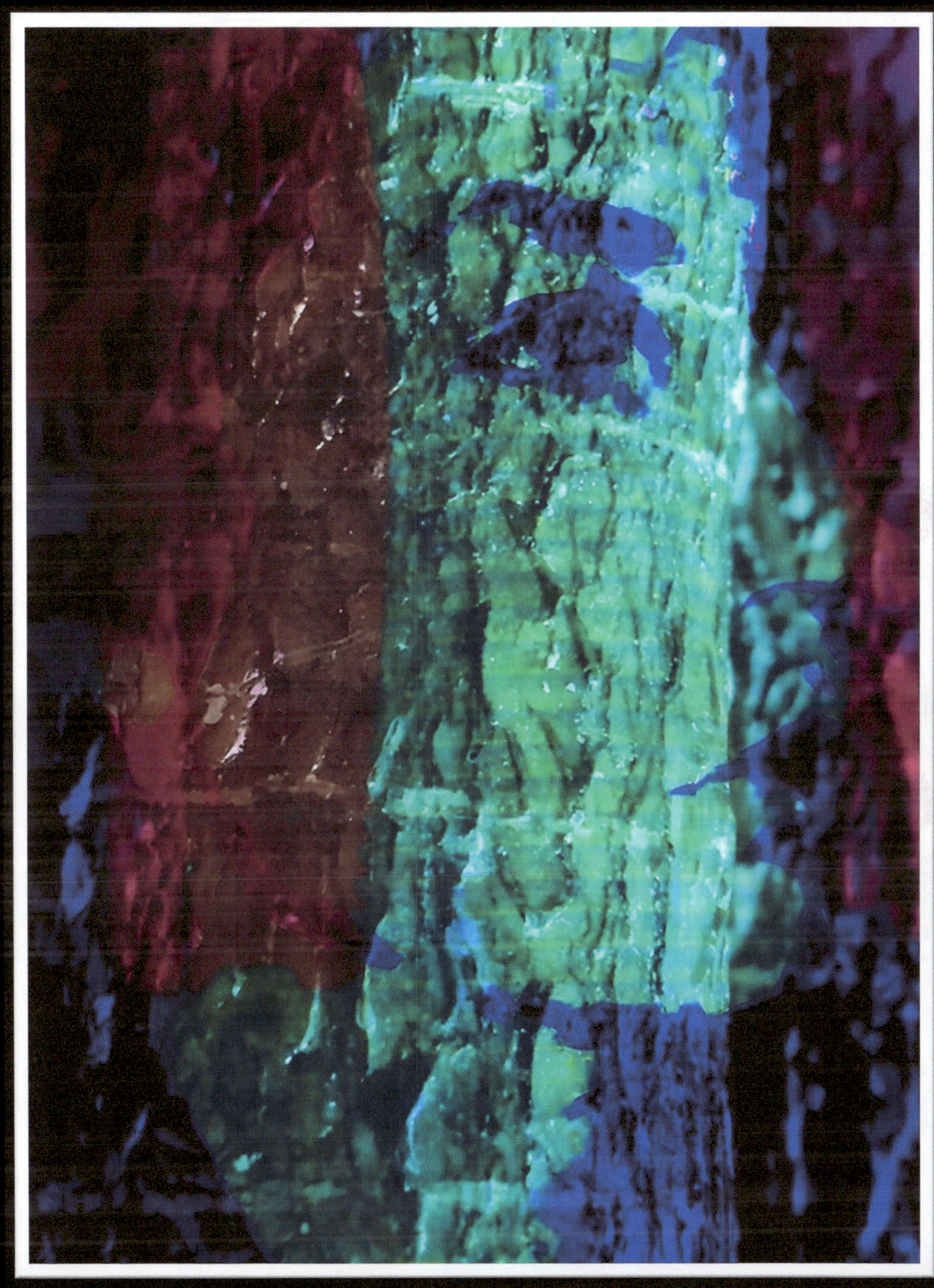

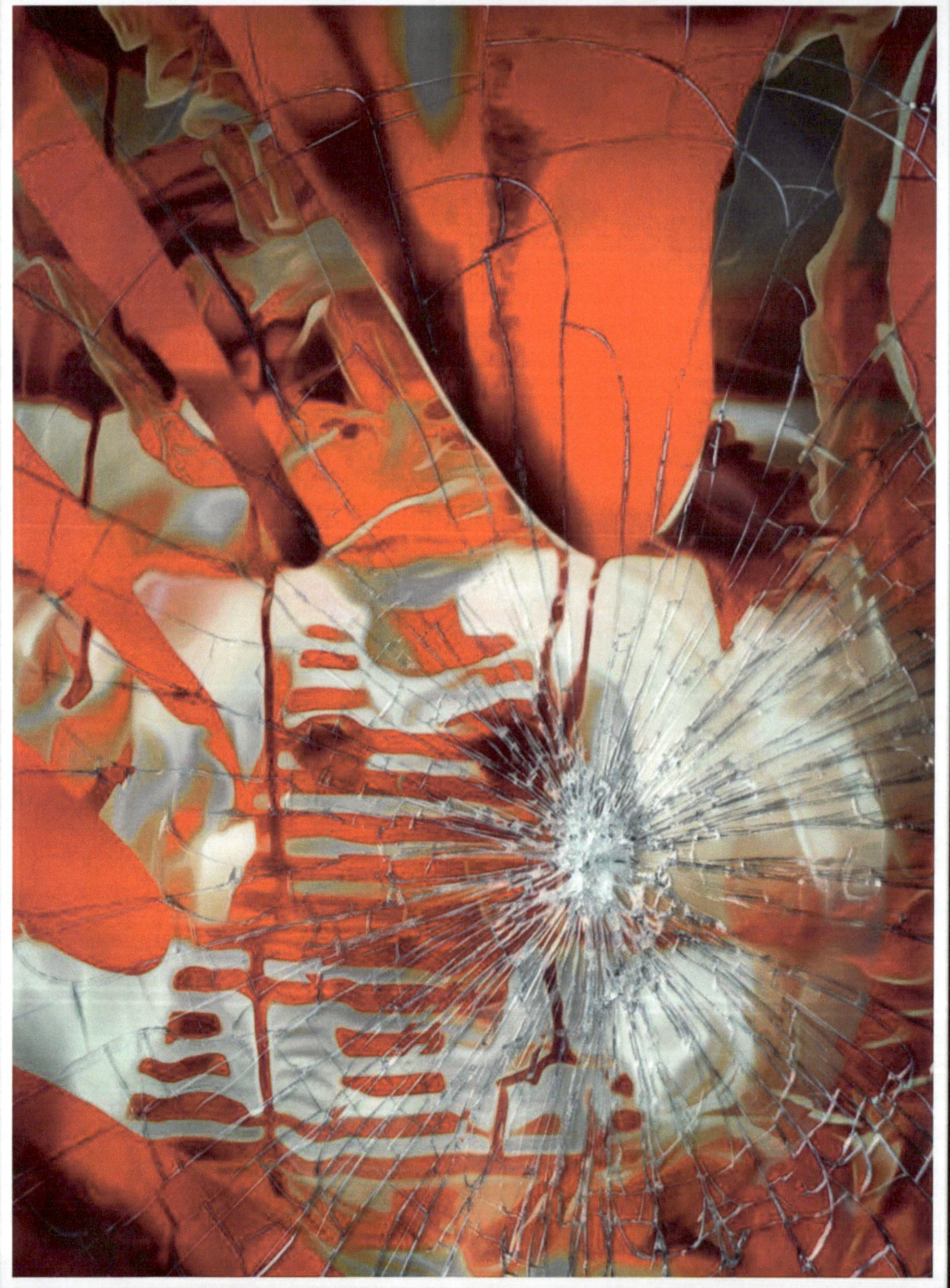

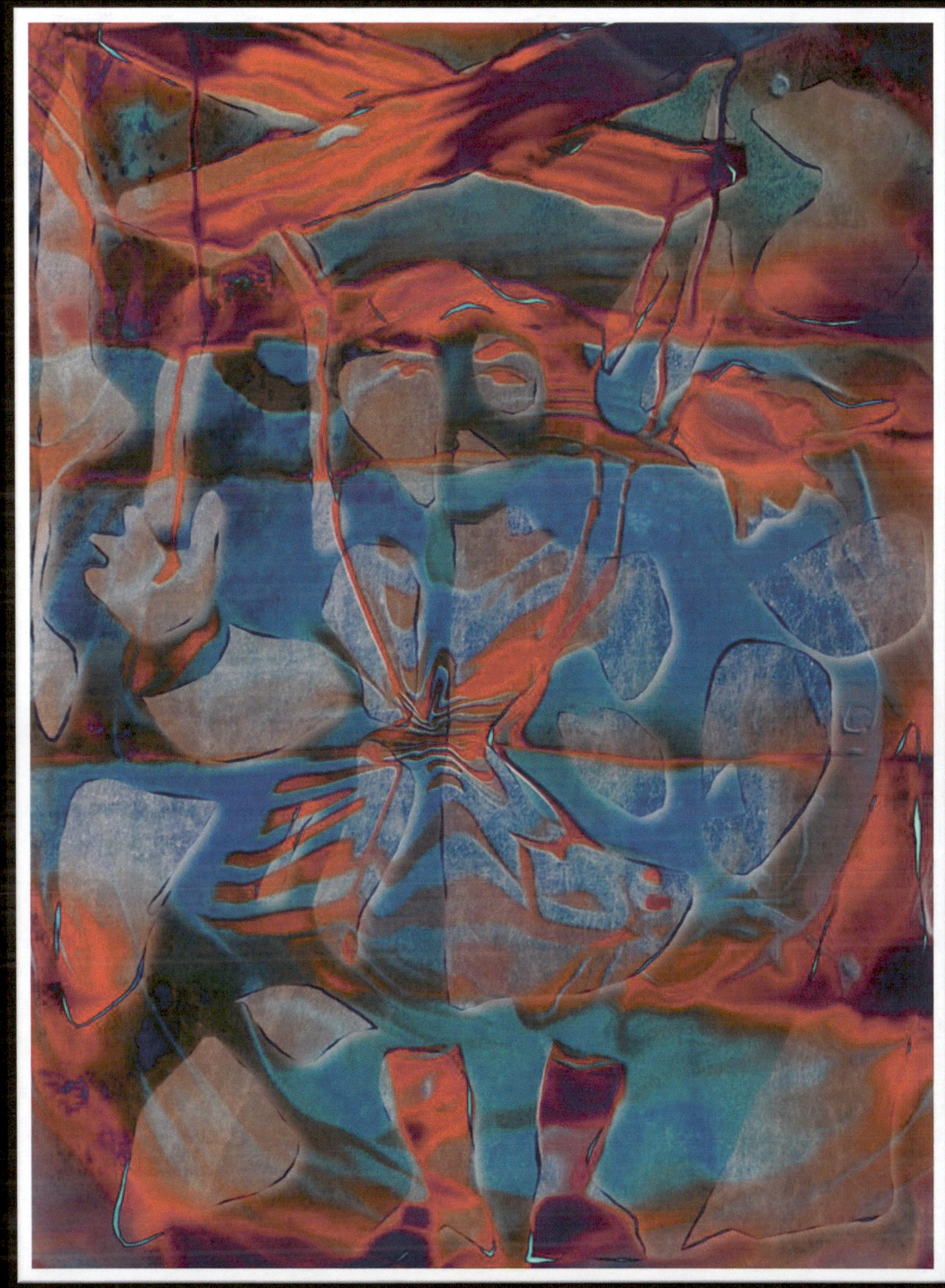

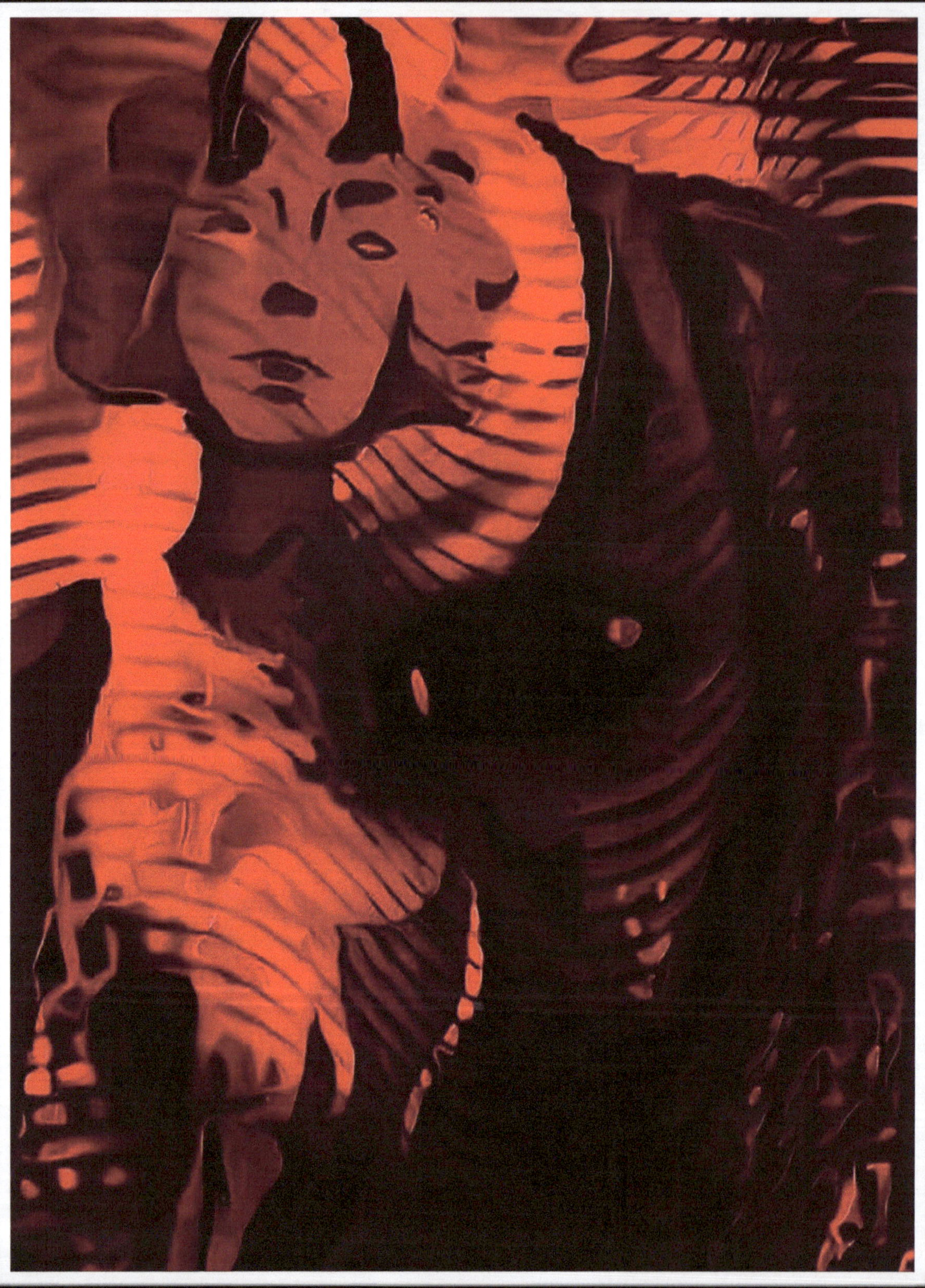

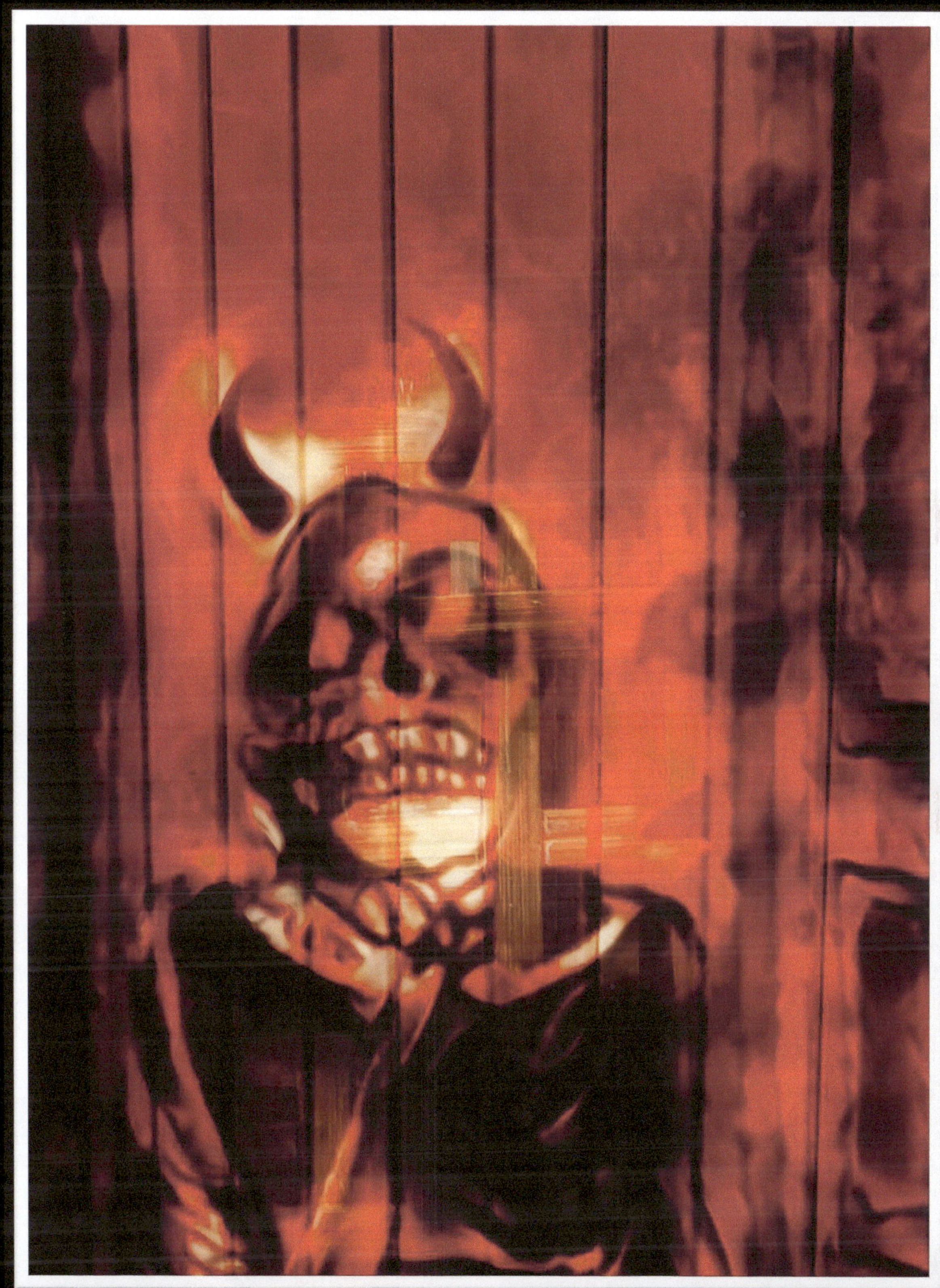

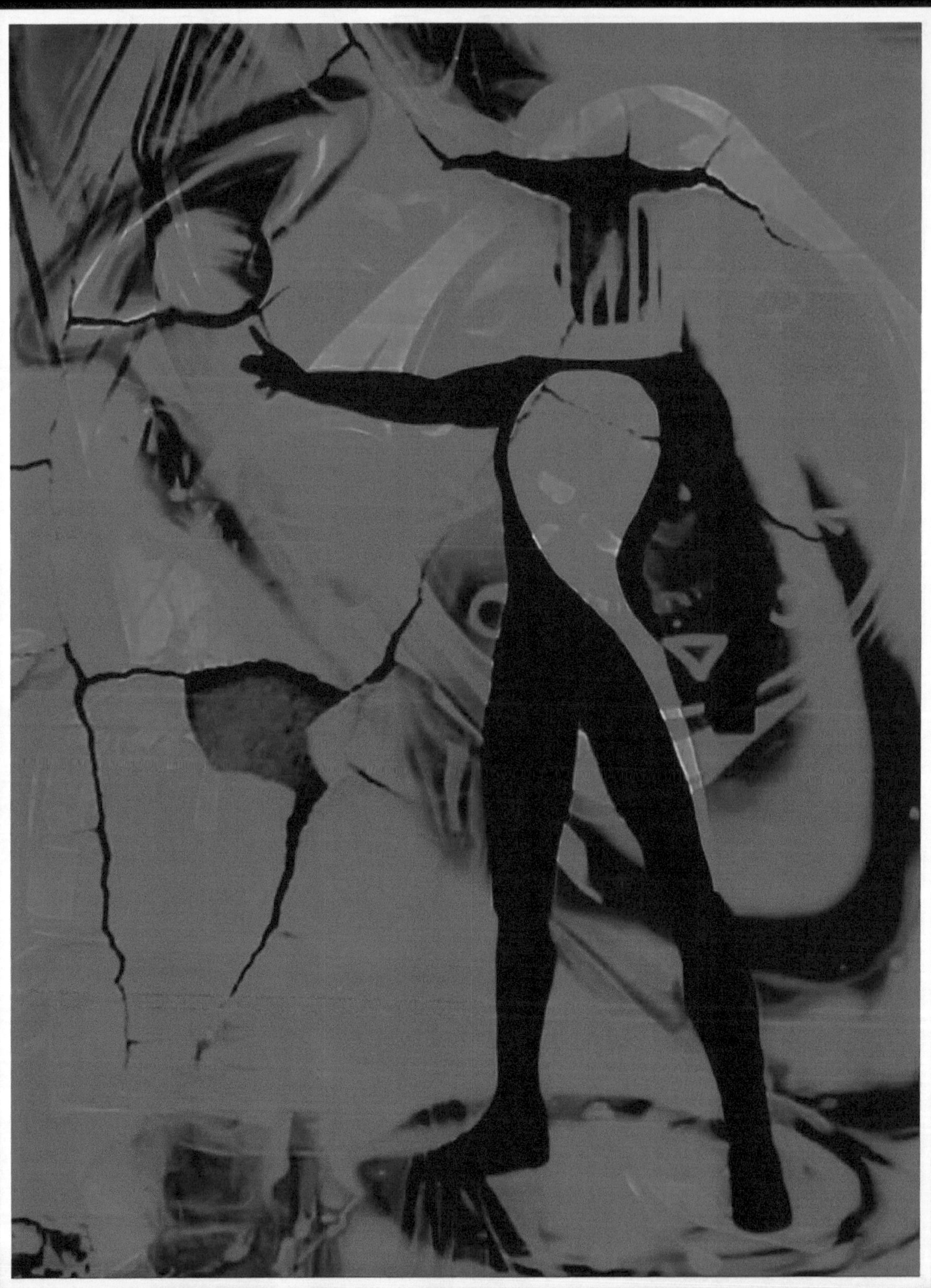

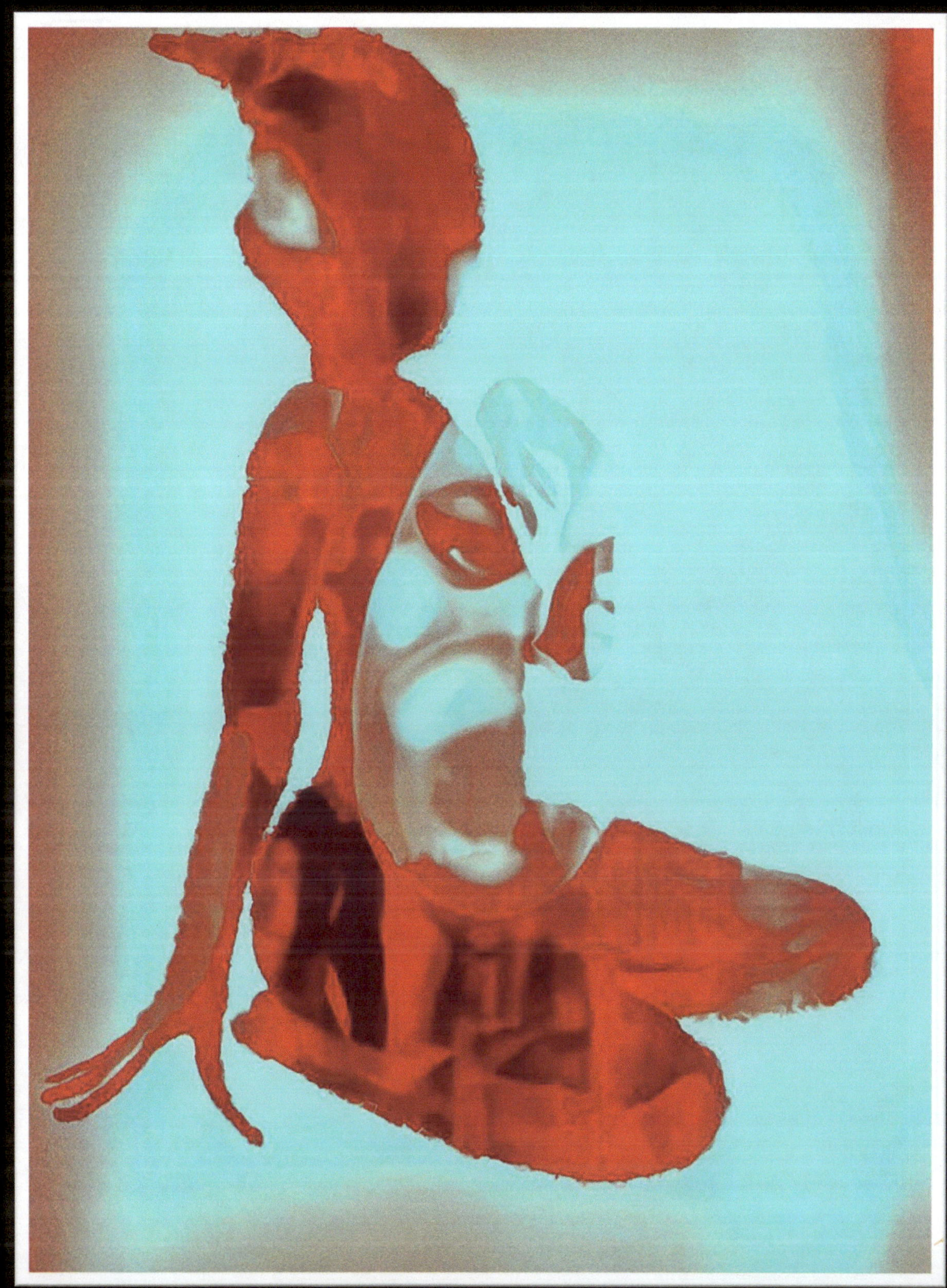

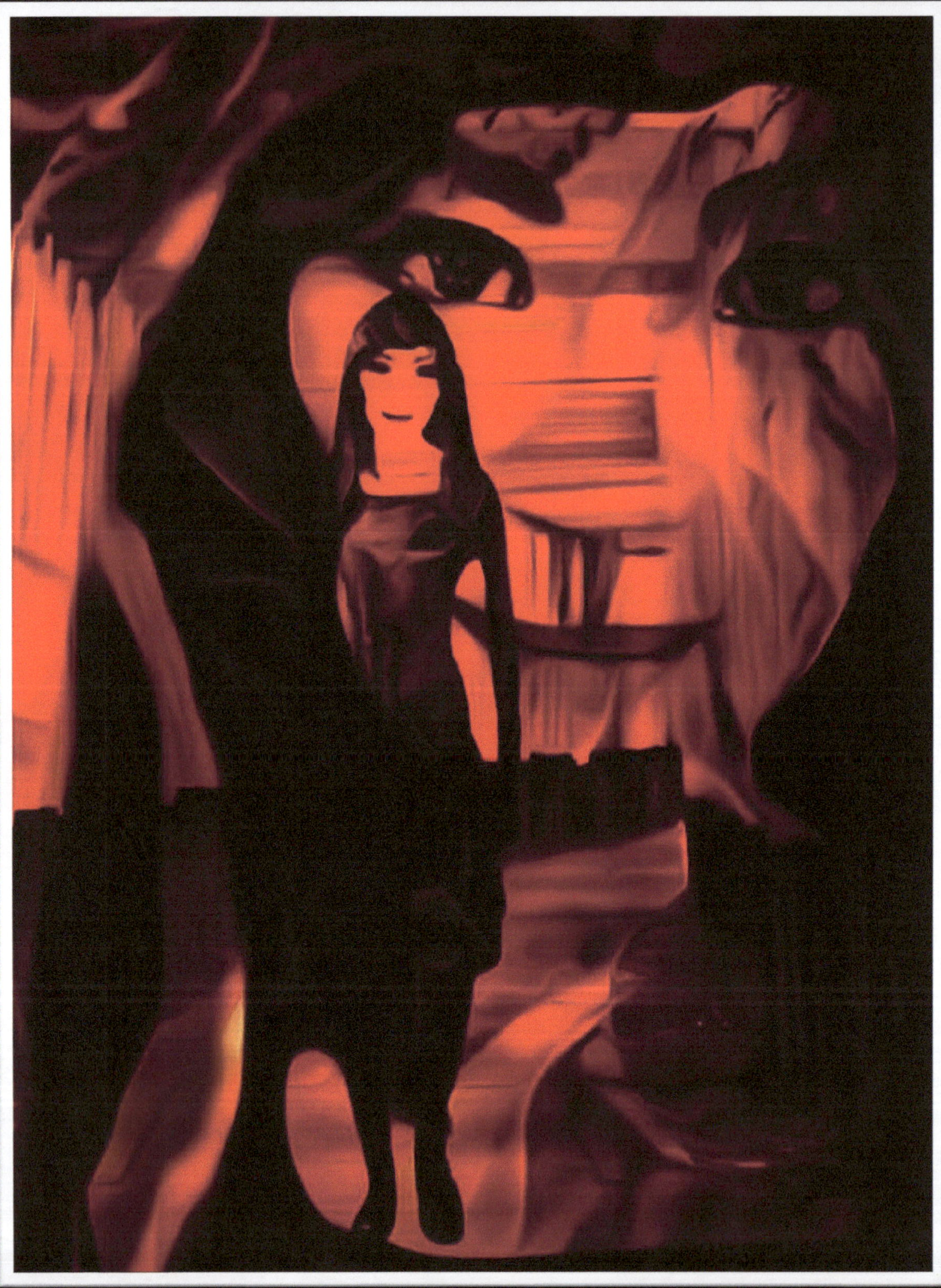

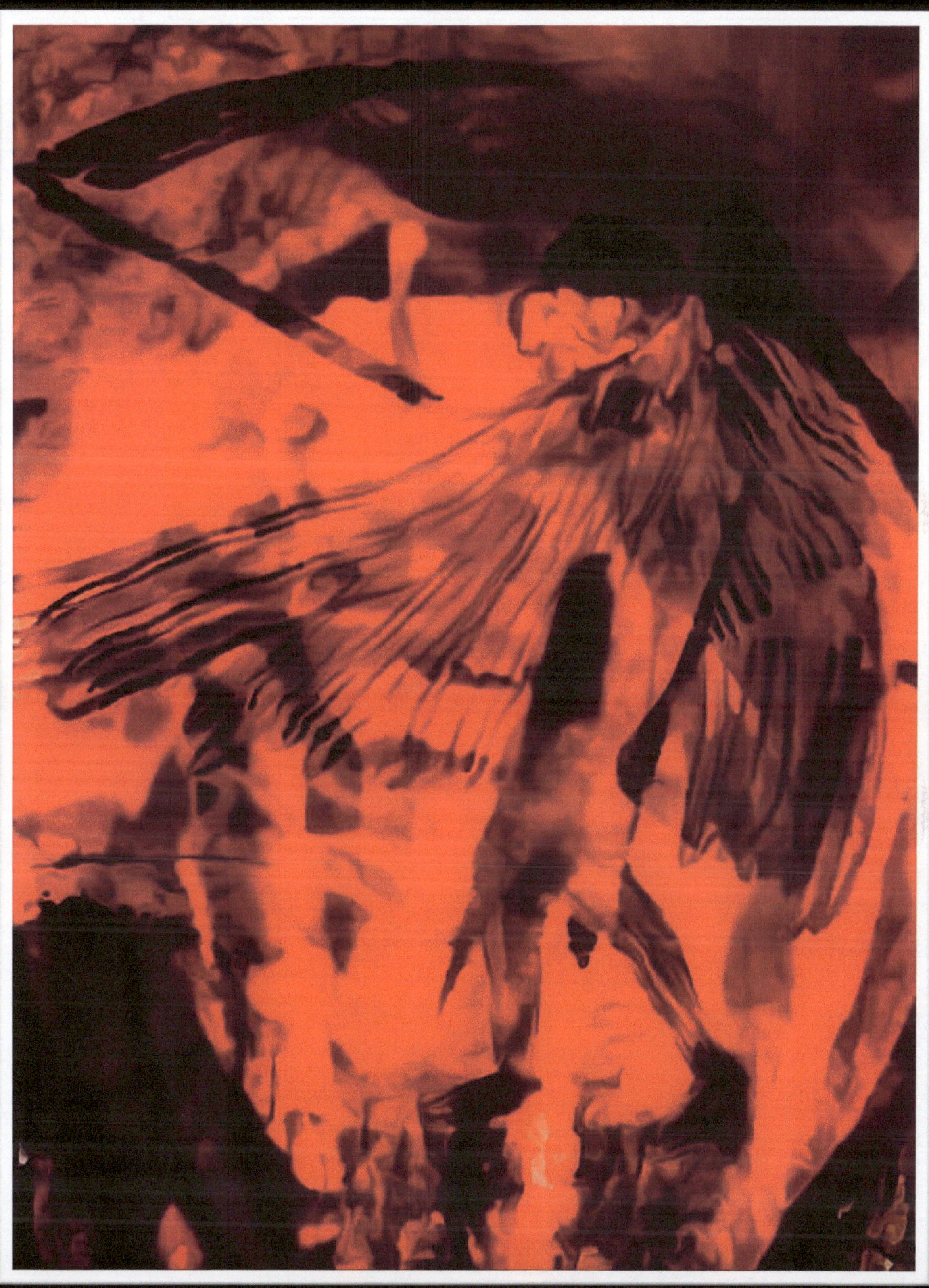

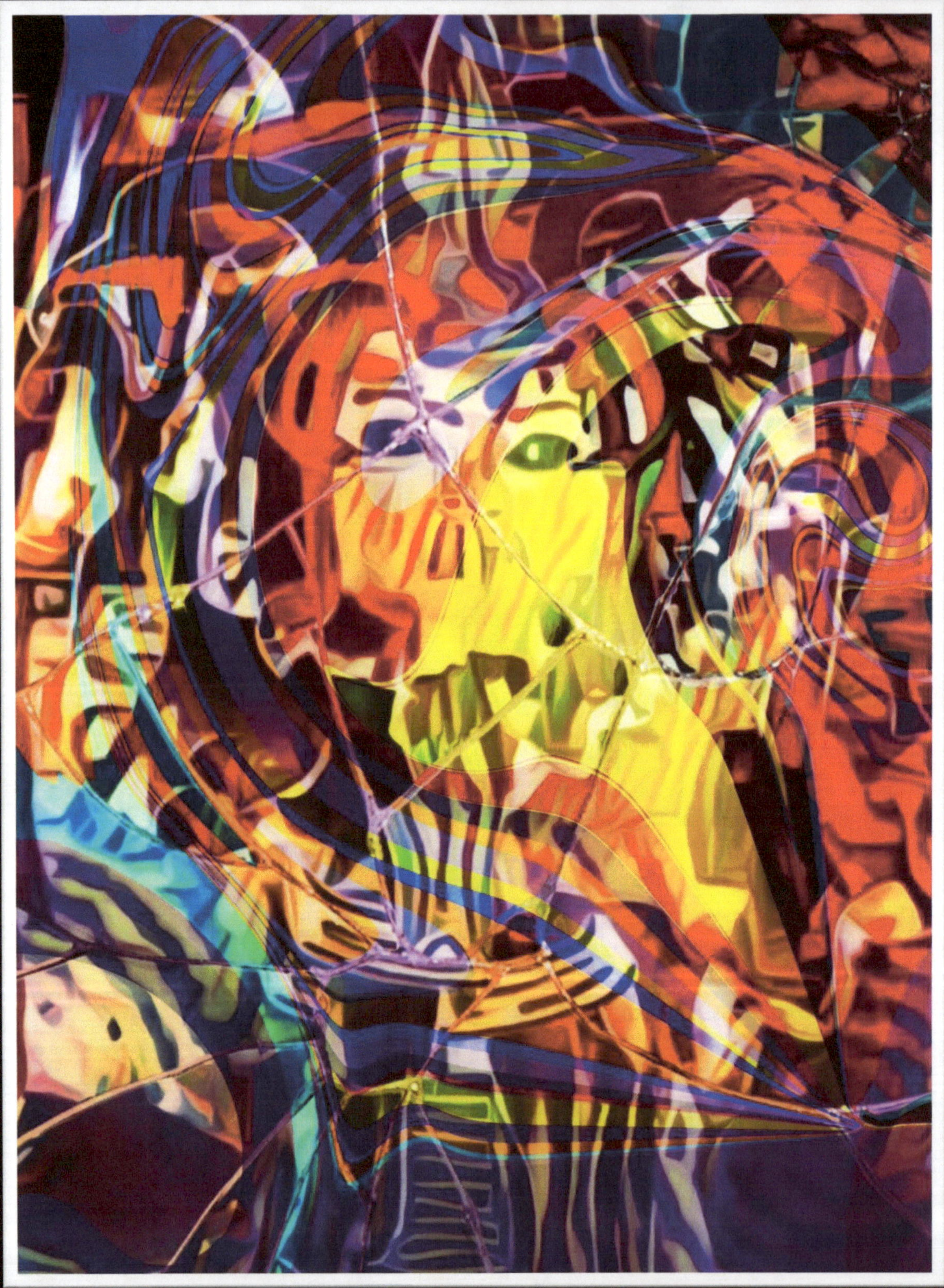

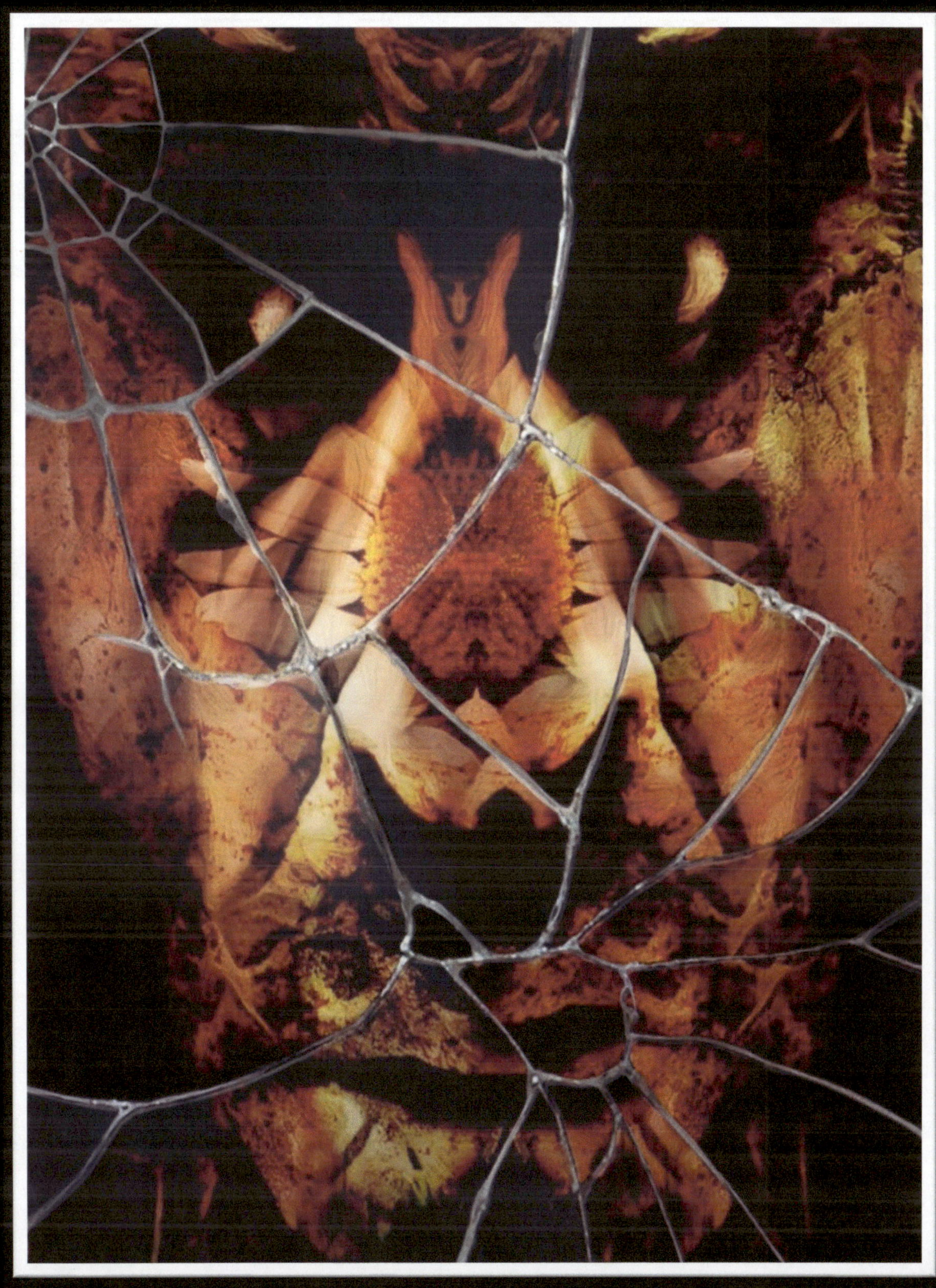

Alycia Hodge

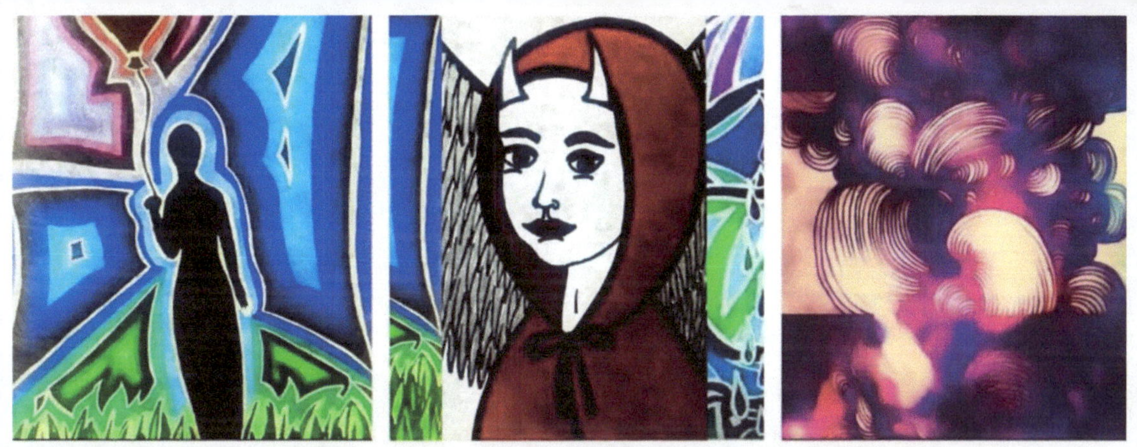

About Alycia Hodge

Alycia Hodge is a writer, artist and editor living in the U.S. in Oregon. She believes writing and art help us to heal and connect with others.

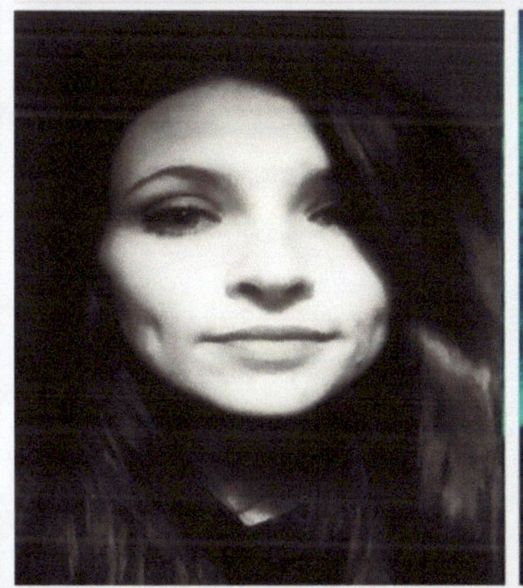

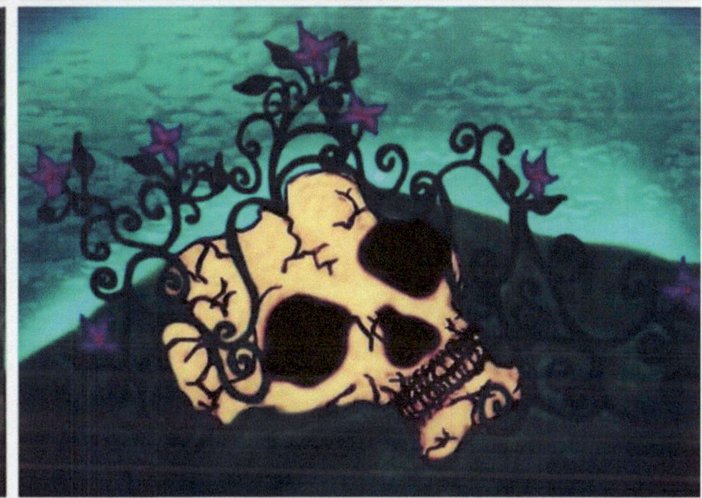

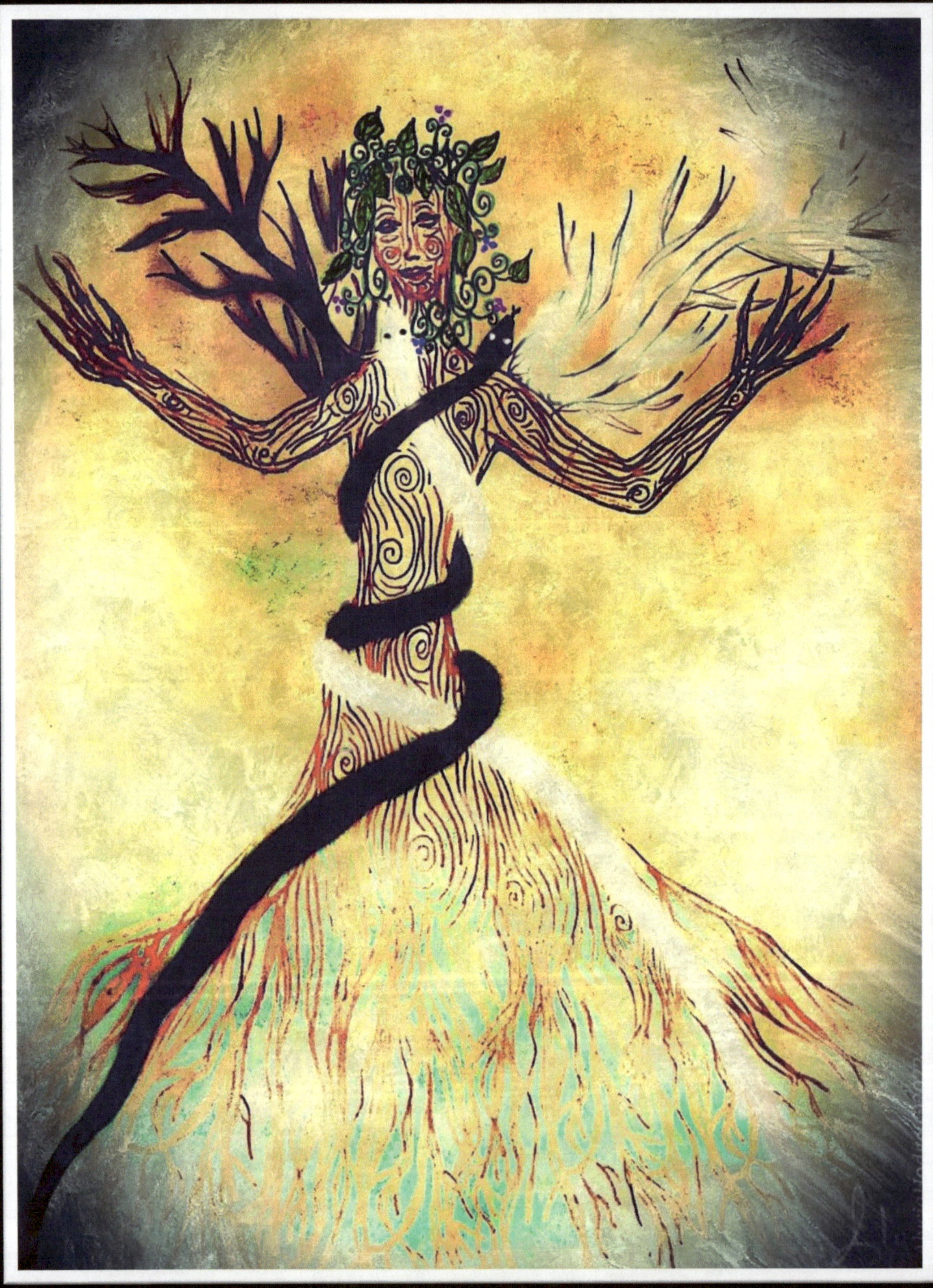

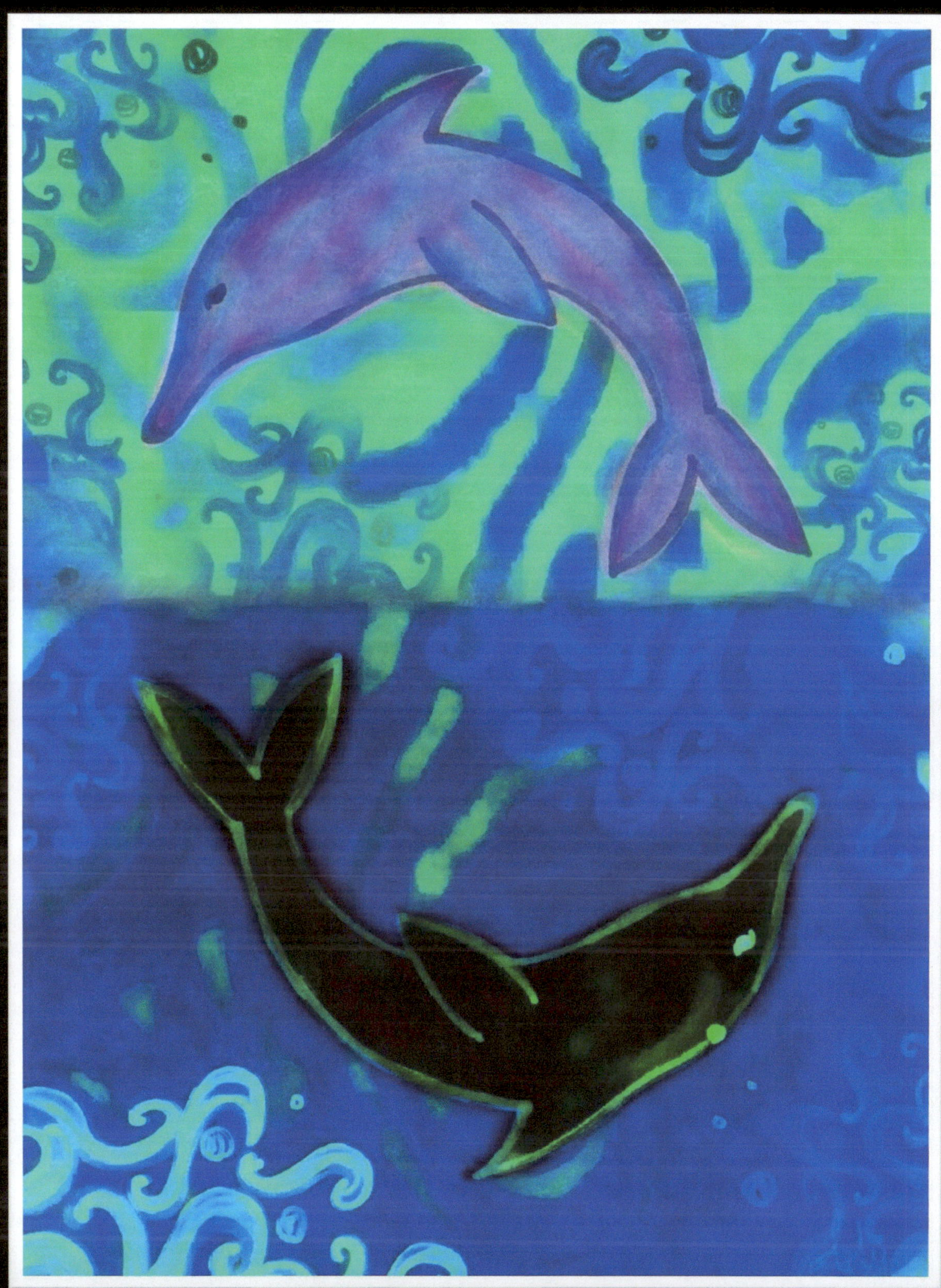

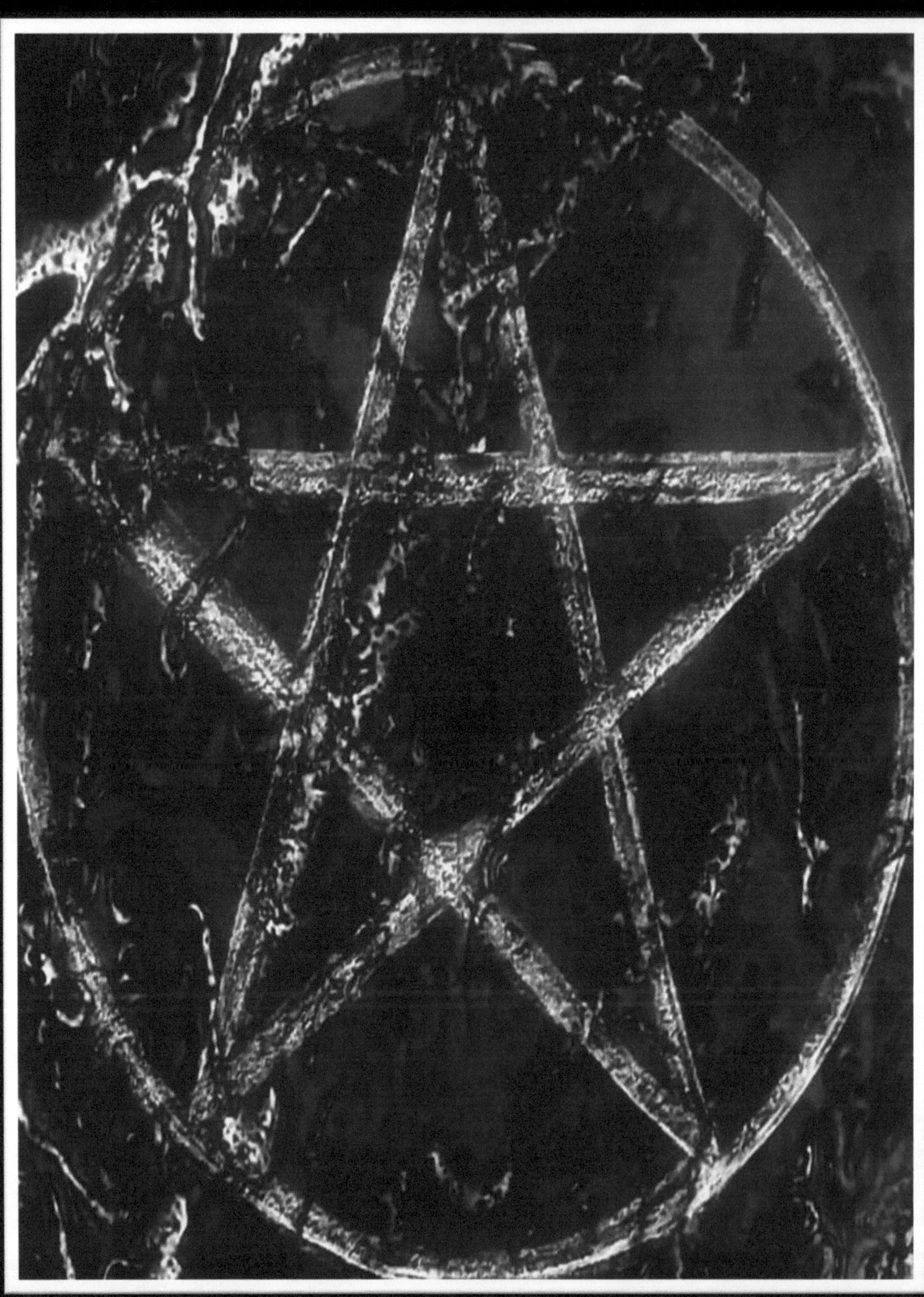

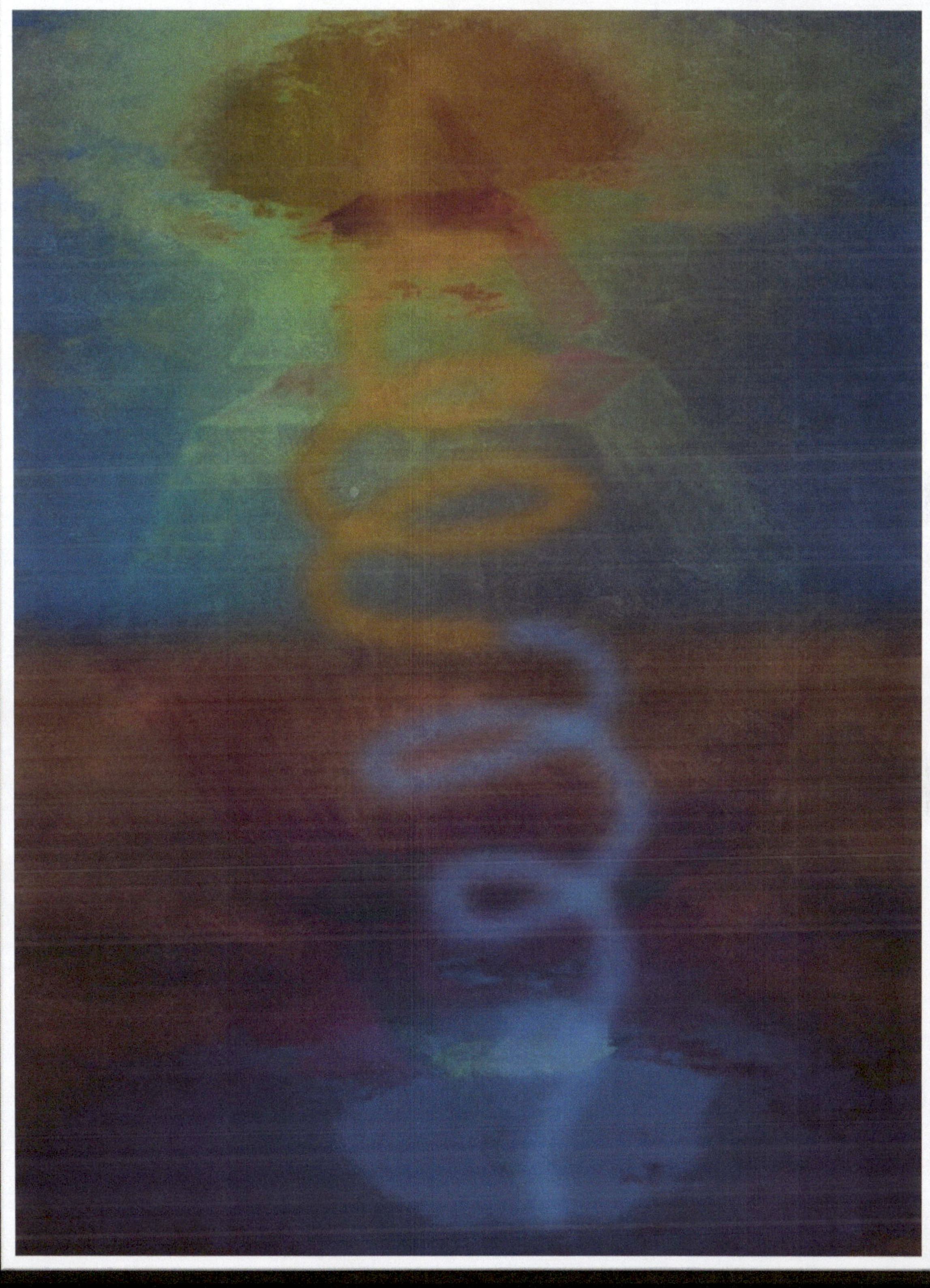

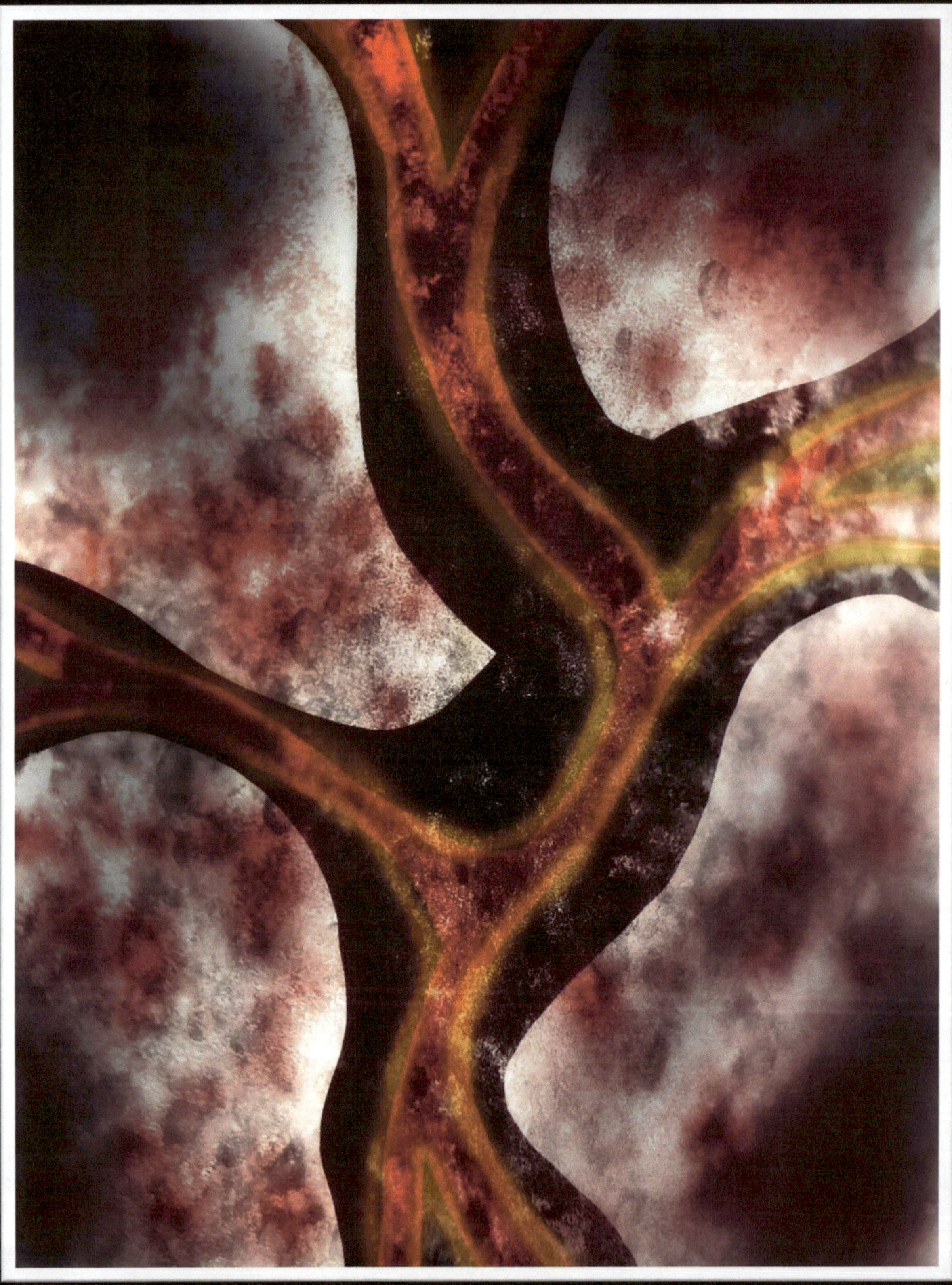

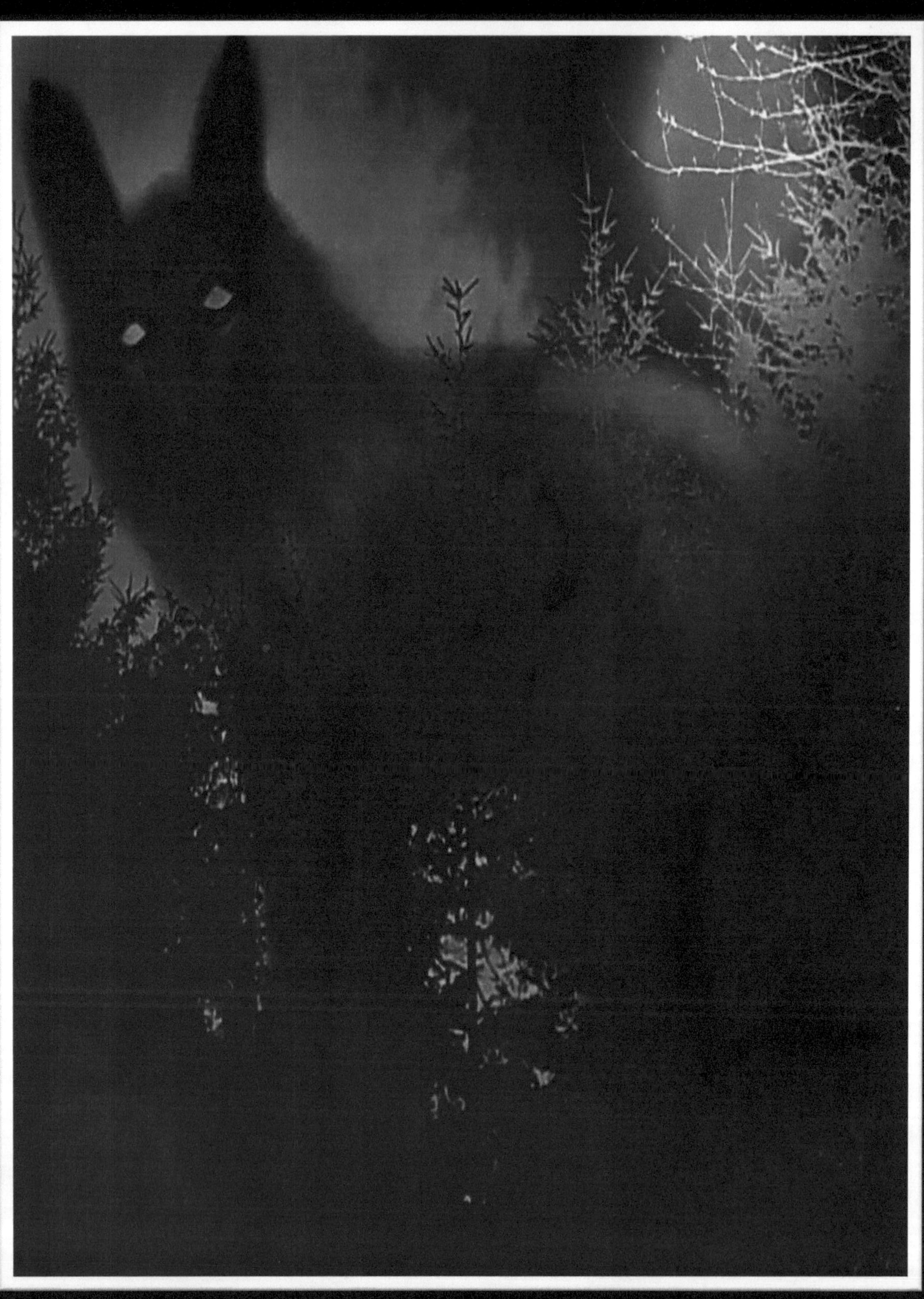

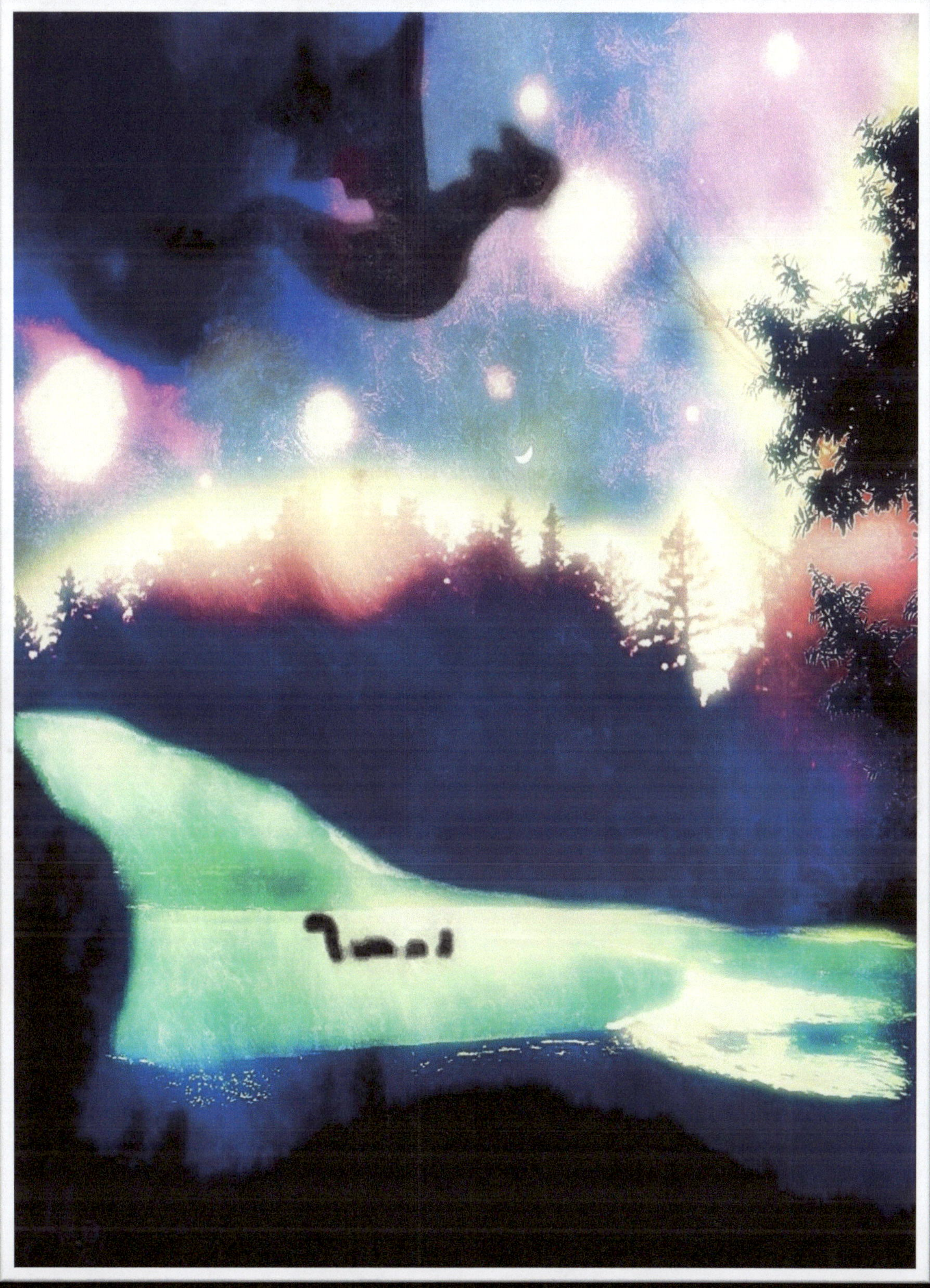

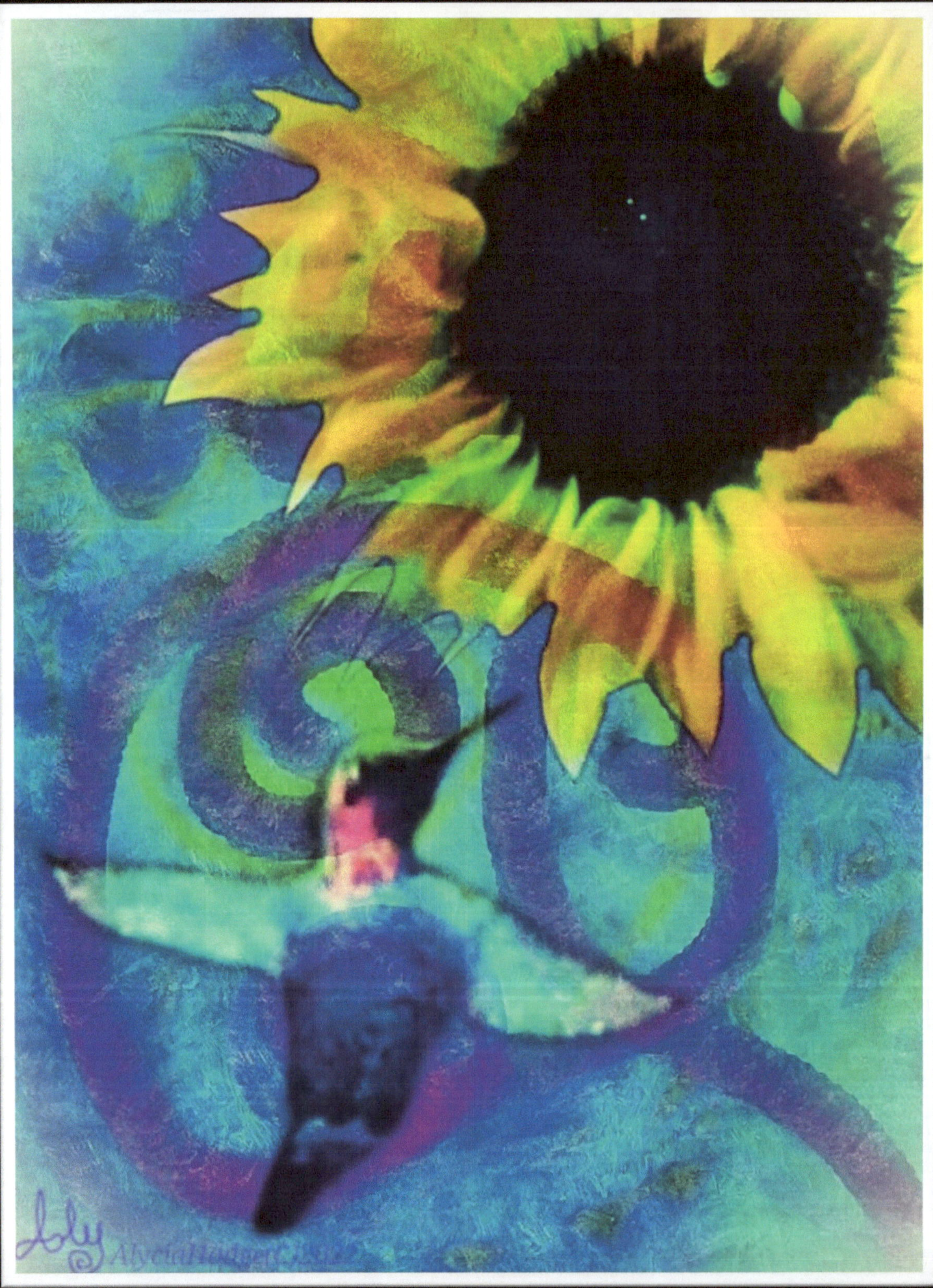

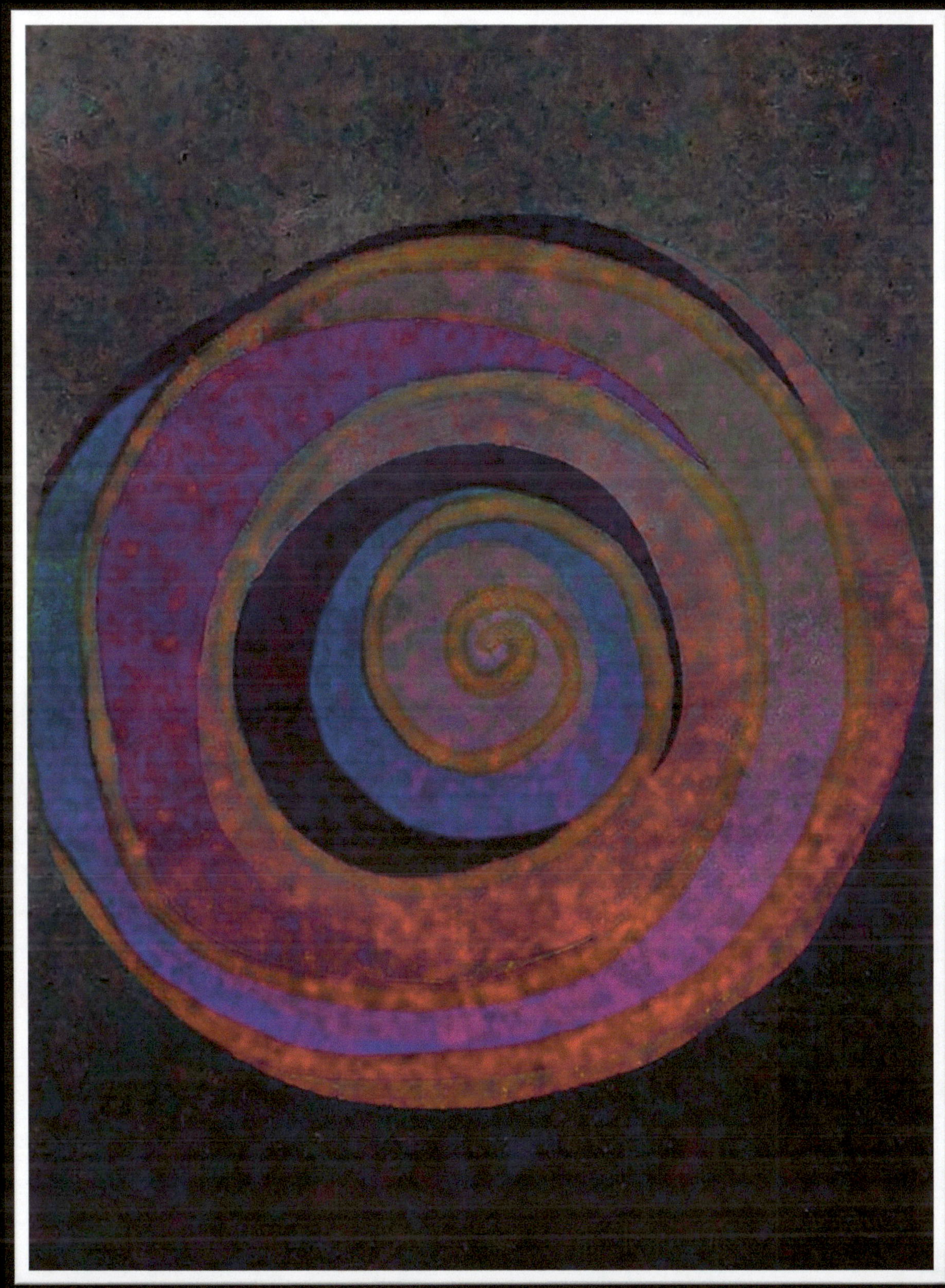

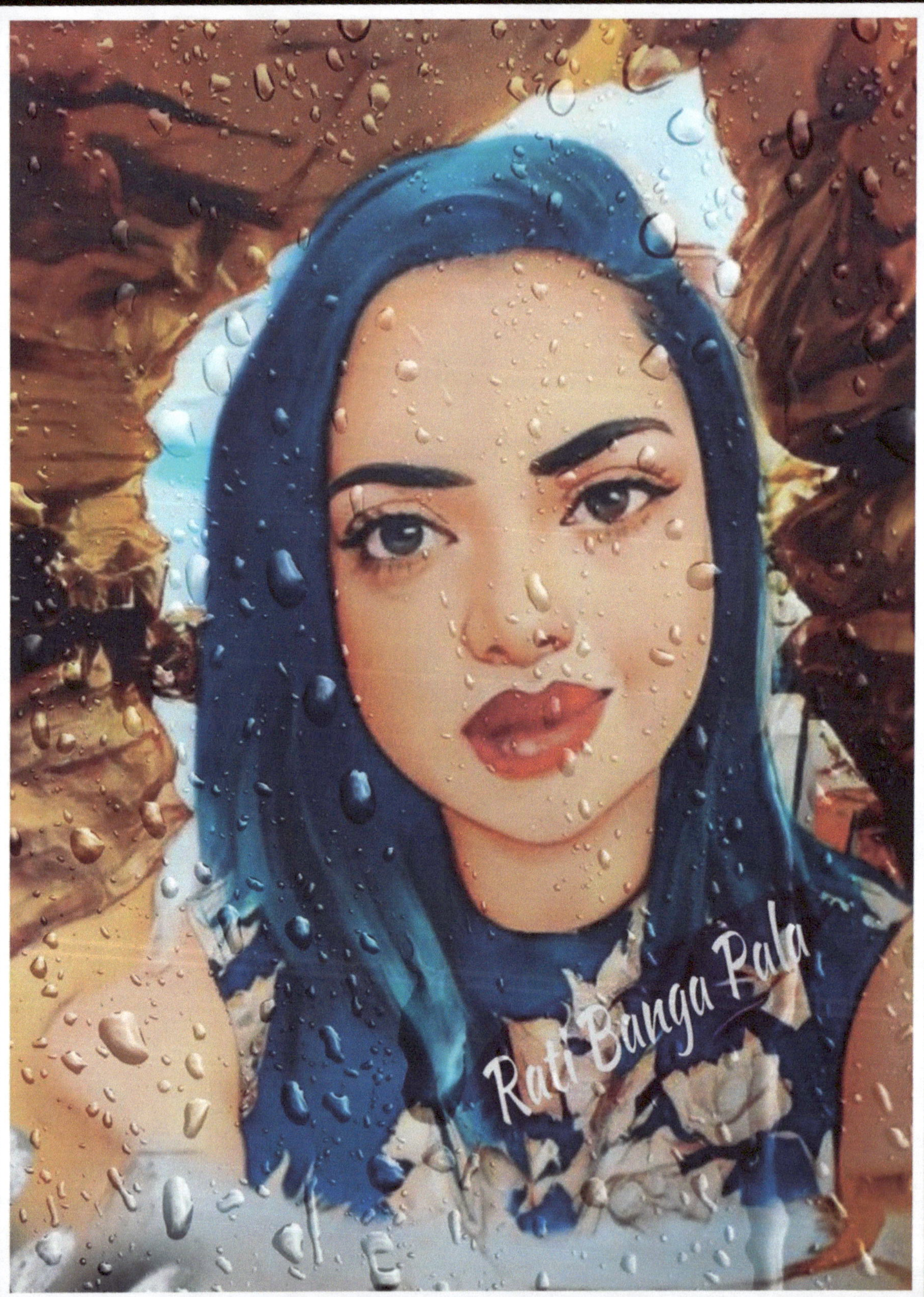
Rati Banga Bala

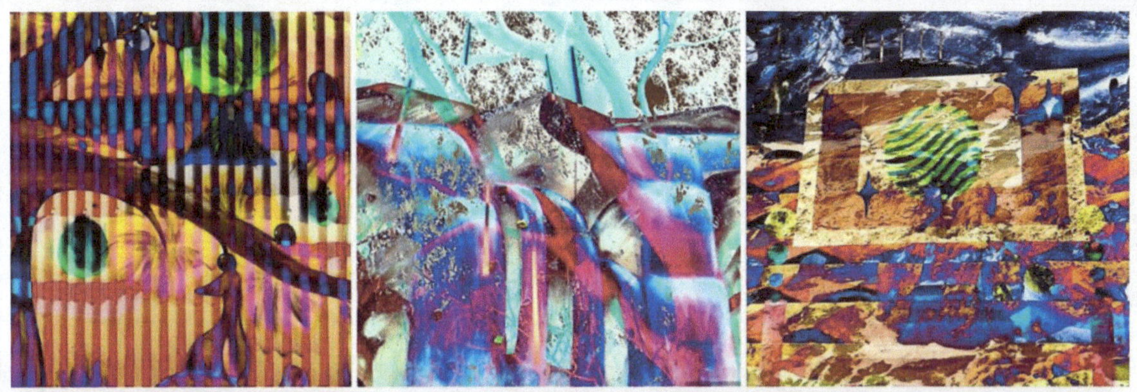

About Rati Banga Pala

Rati is a published writer, photographer and artist from Melbourne, Australia. Rati was born in France and loves travelling. She is a warrior who suffers from long term chronic illness but believes in living and enjoying life fully. She writes to let her creativity flair, and to express her emotions/thoughts in a safe place. She is married, with two children.

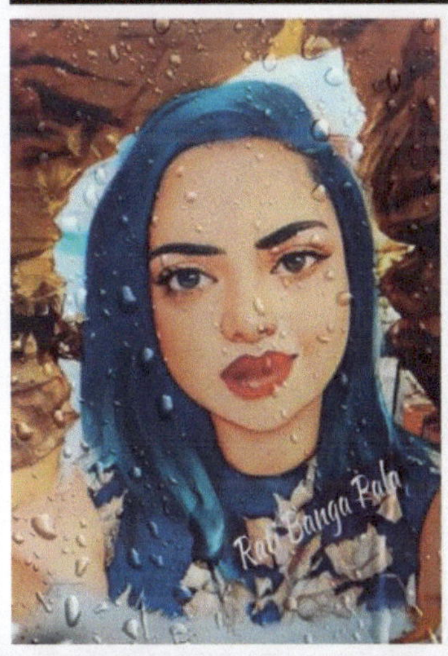

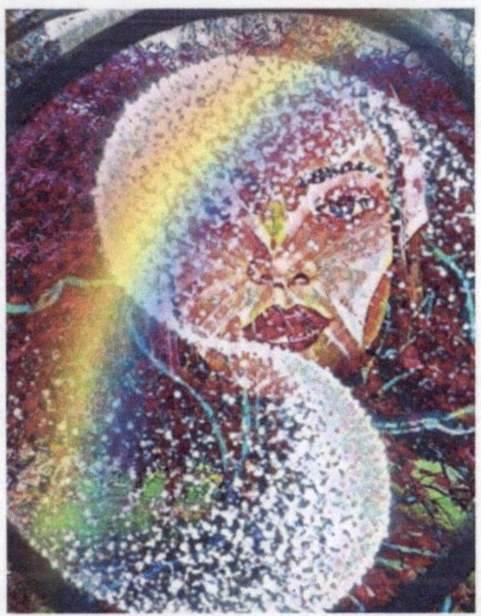

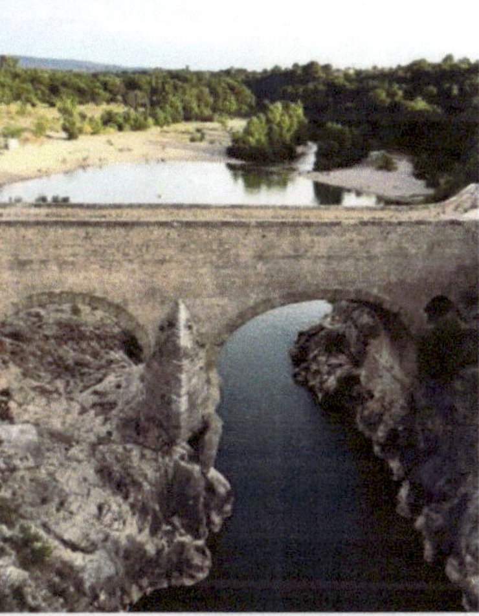

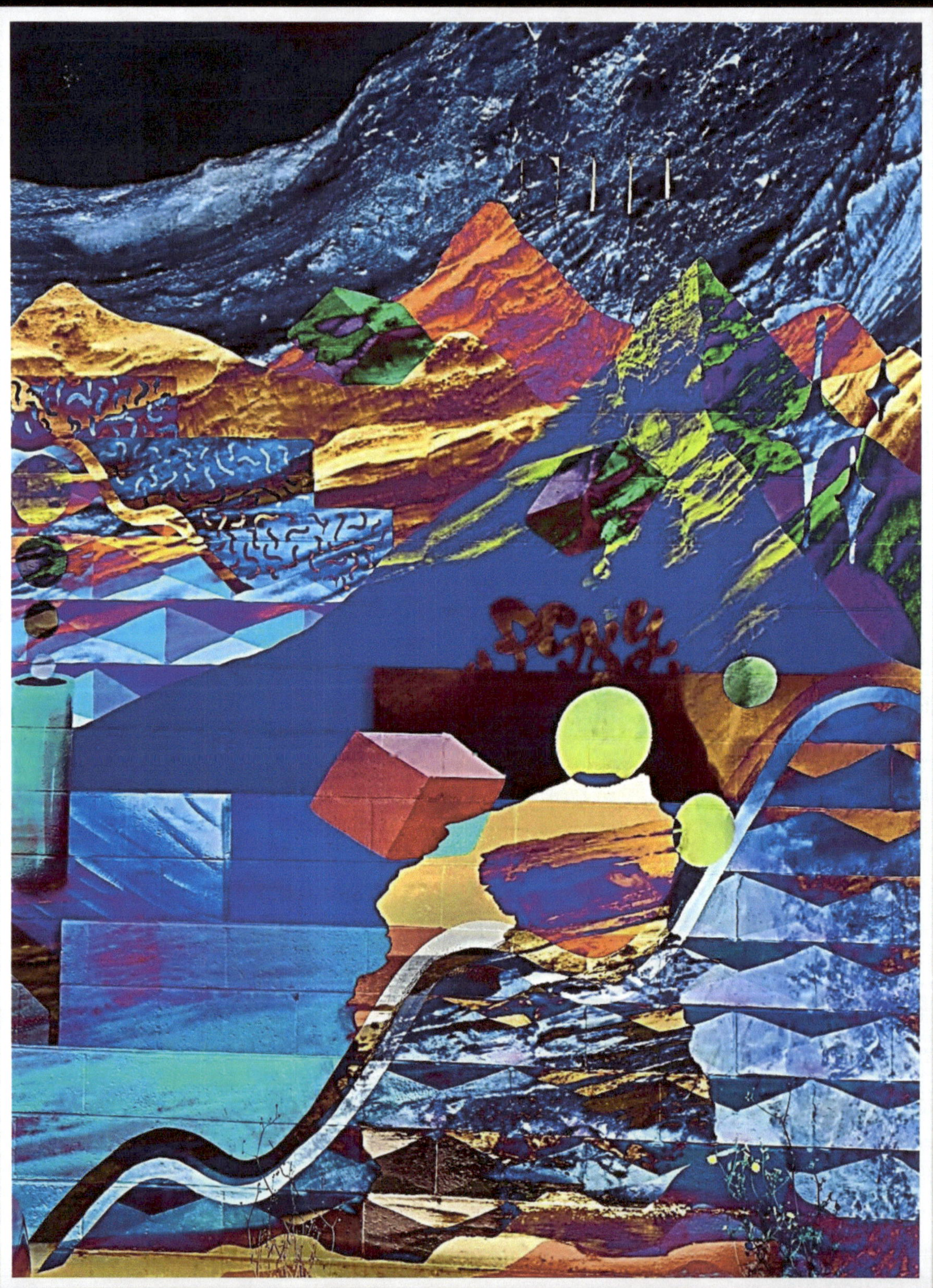

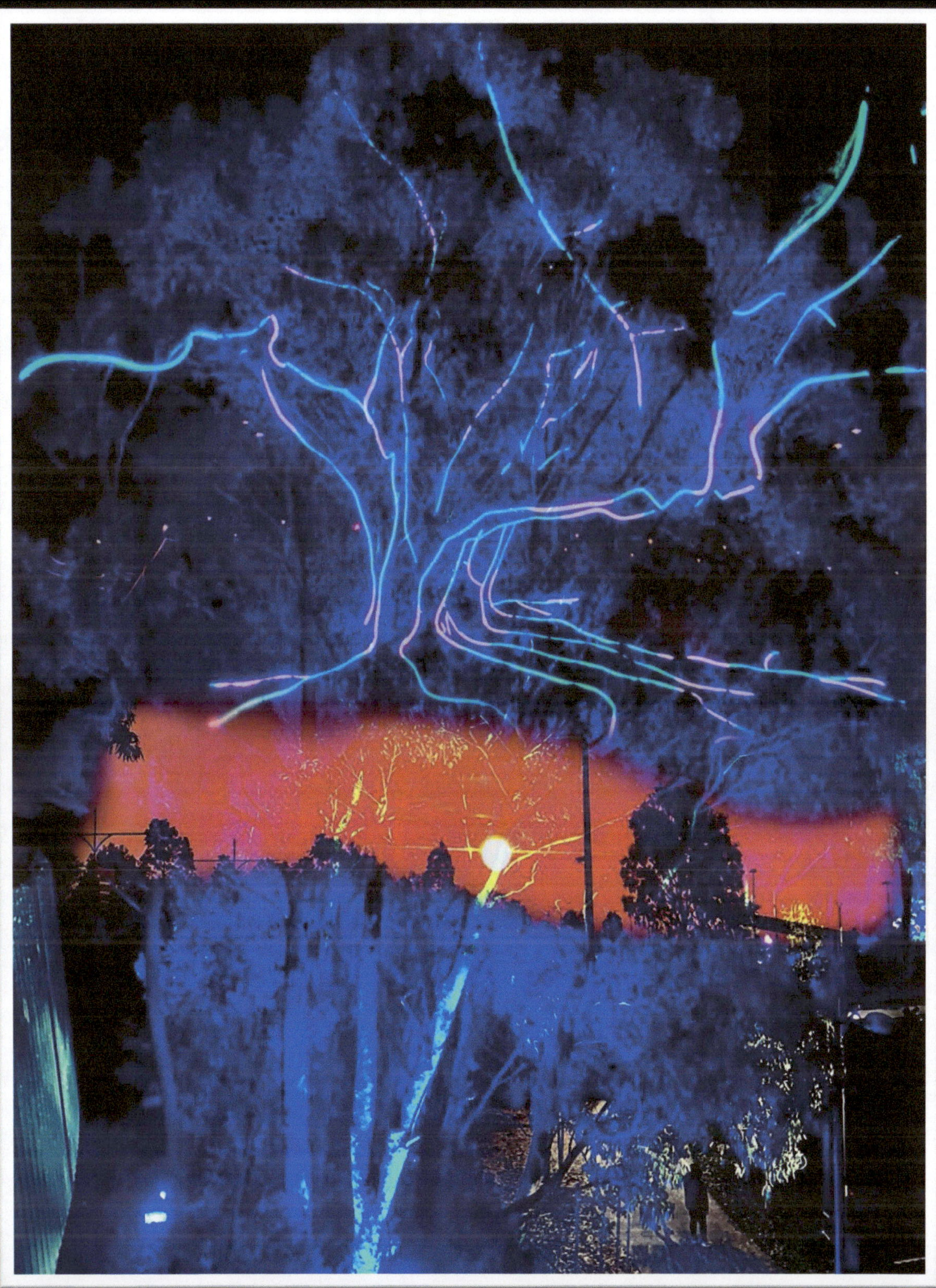

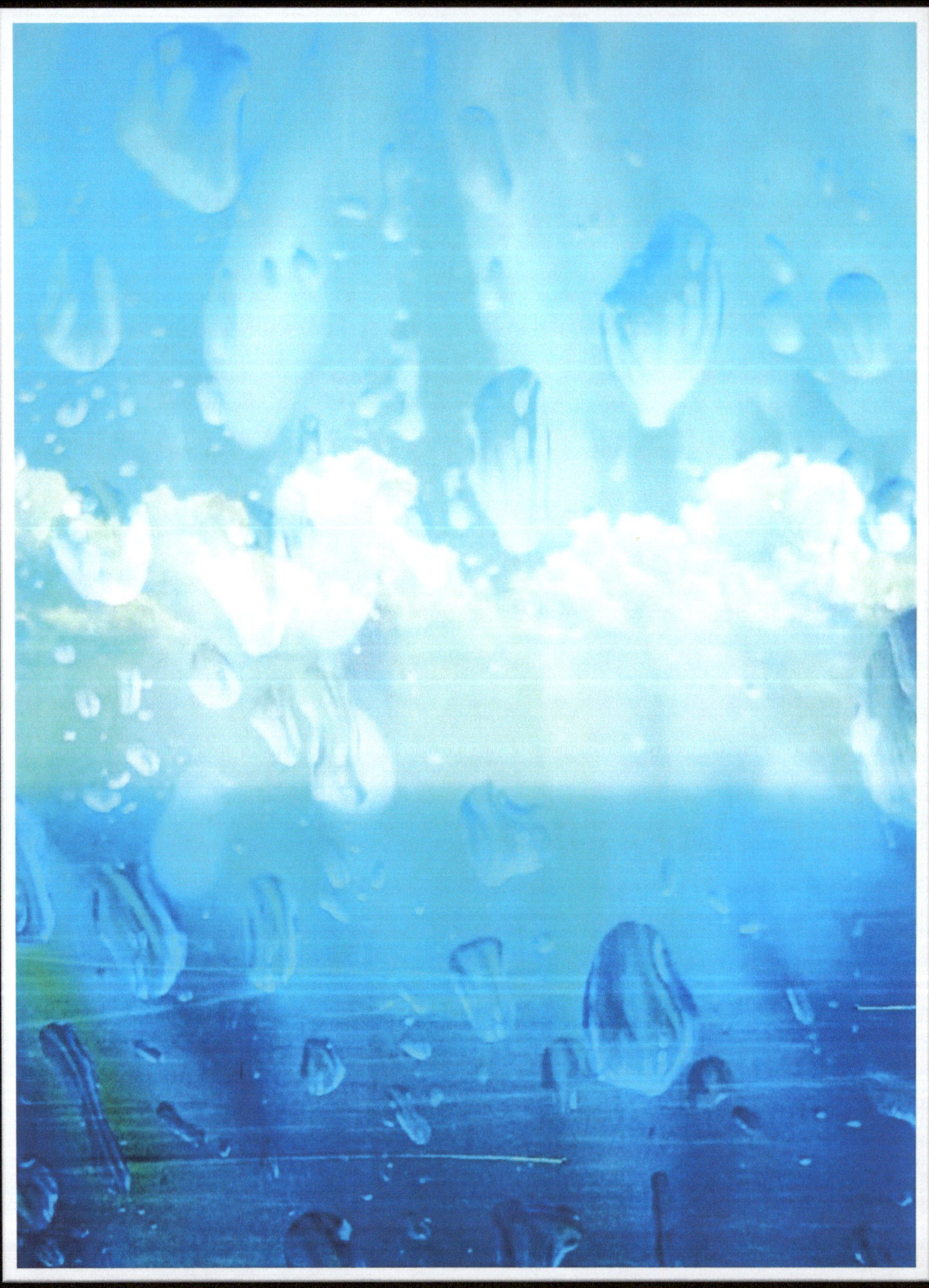

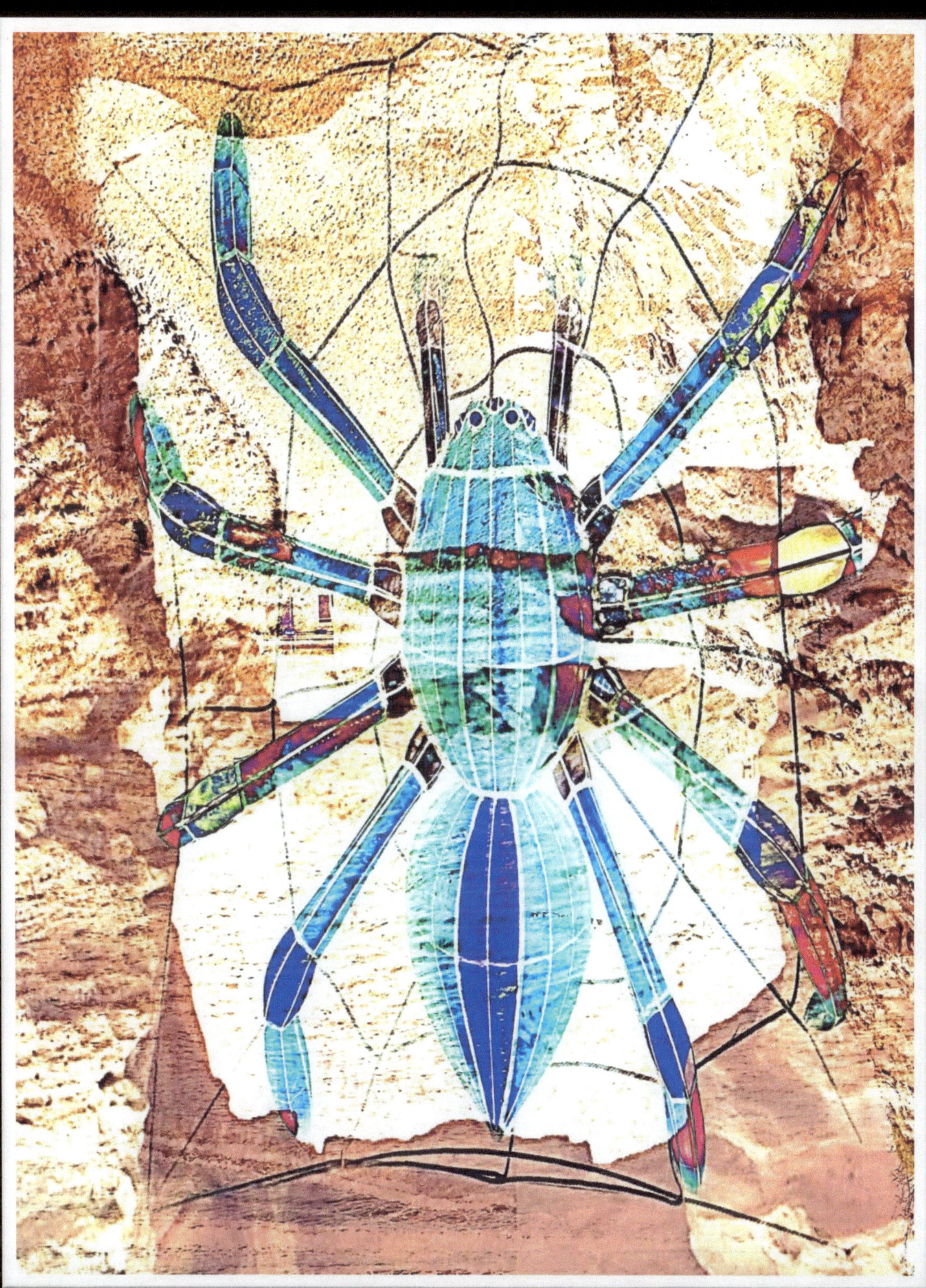

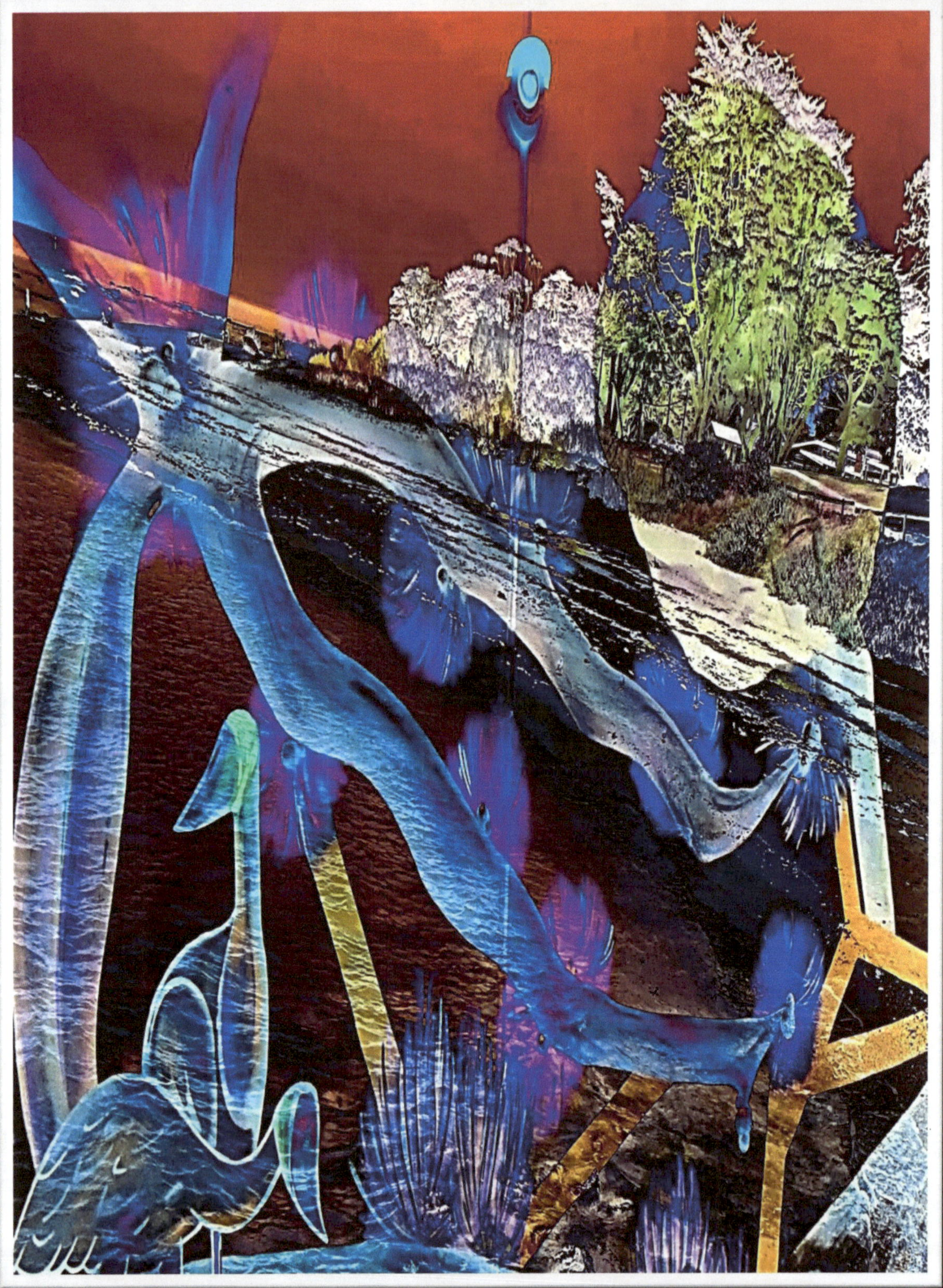

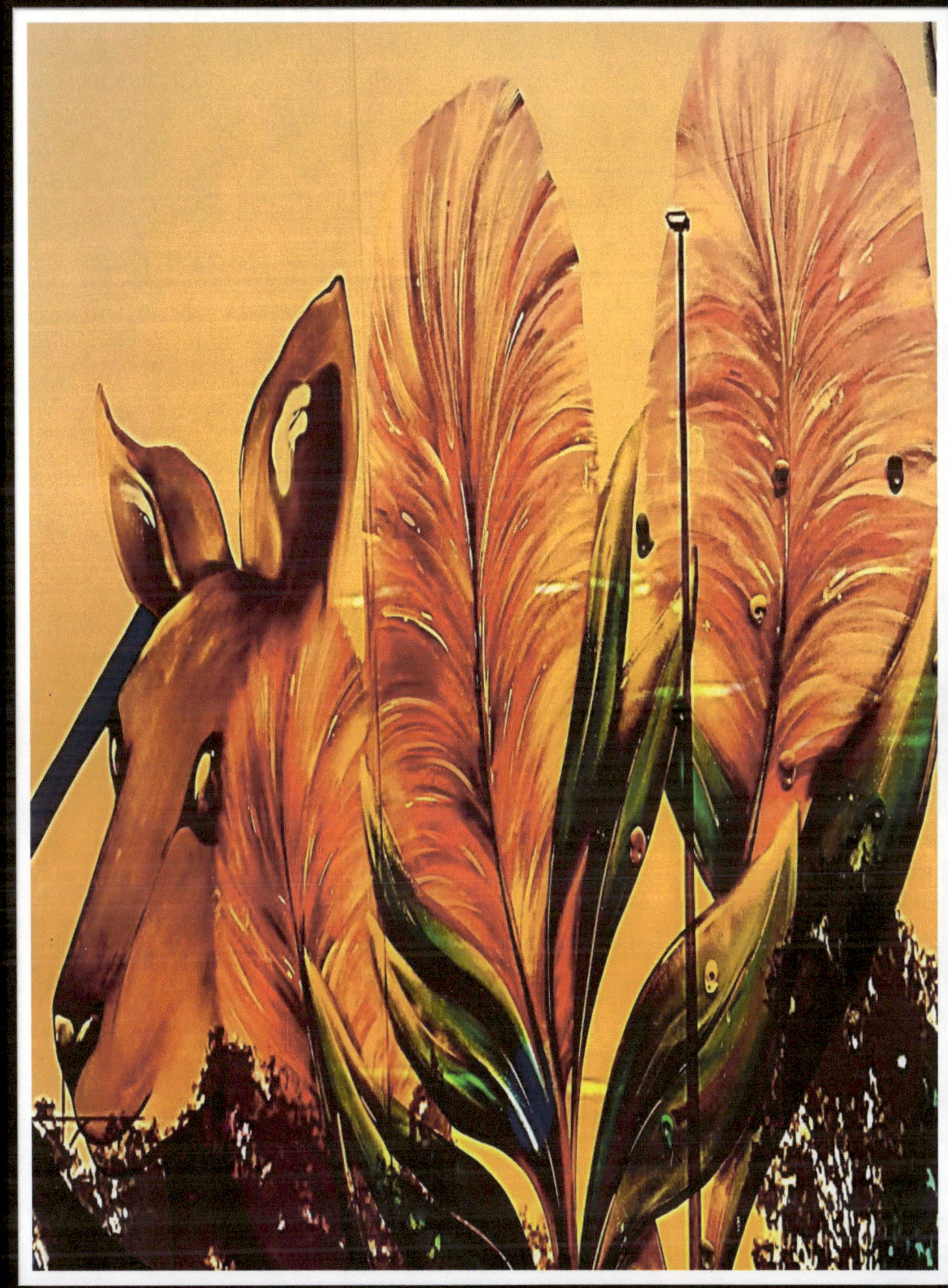

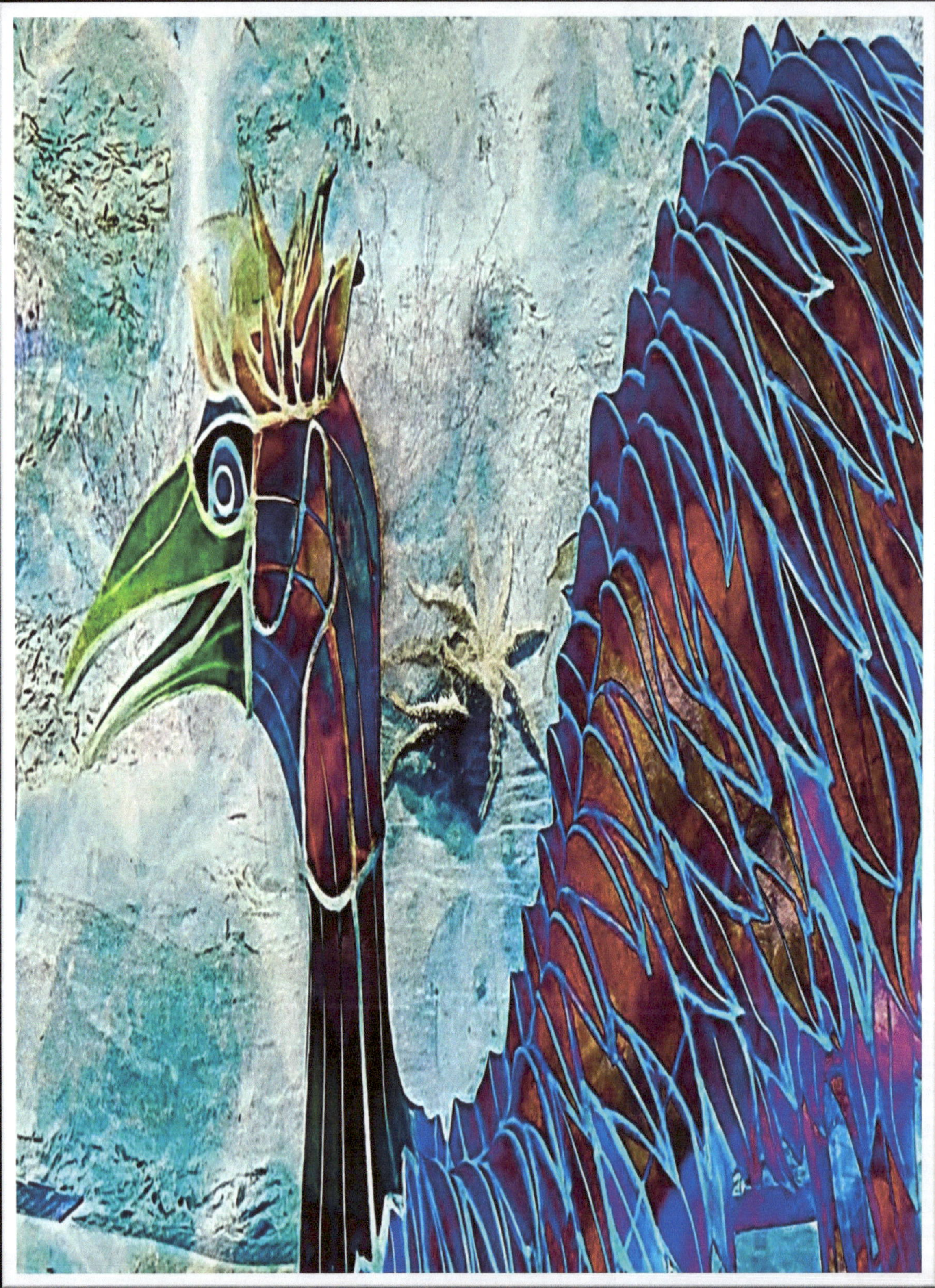

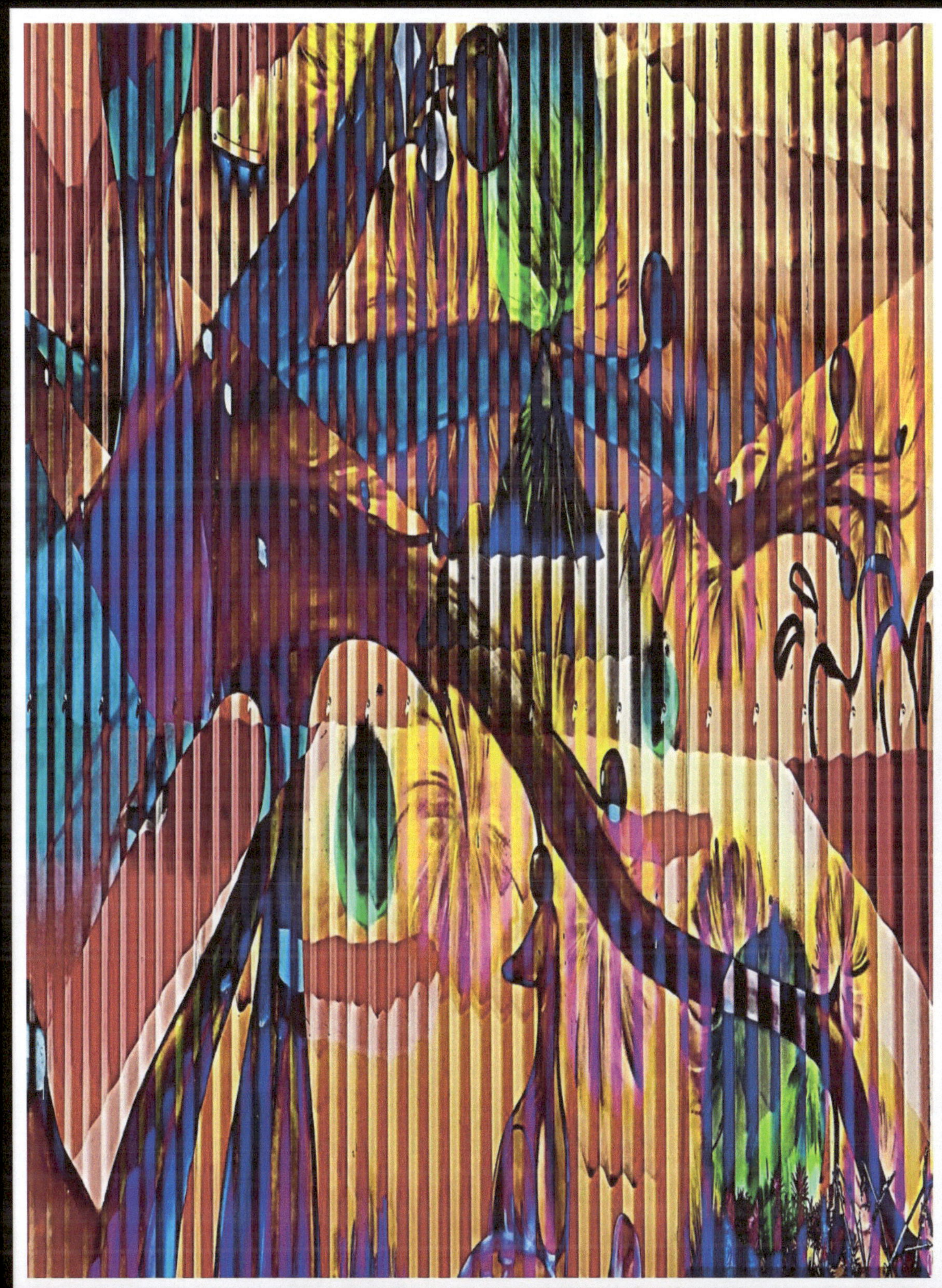

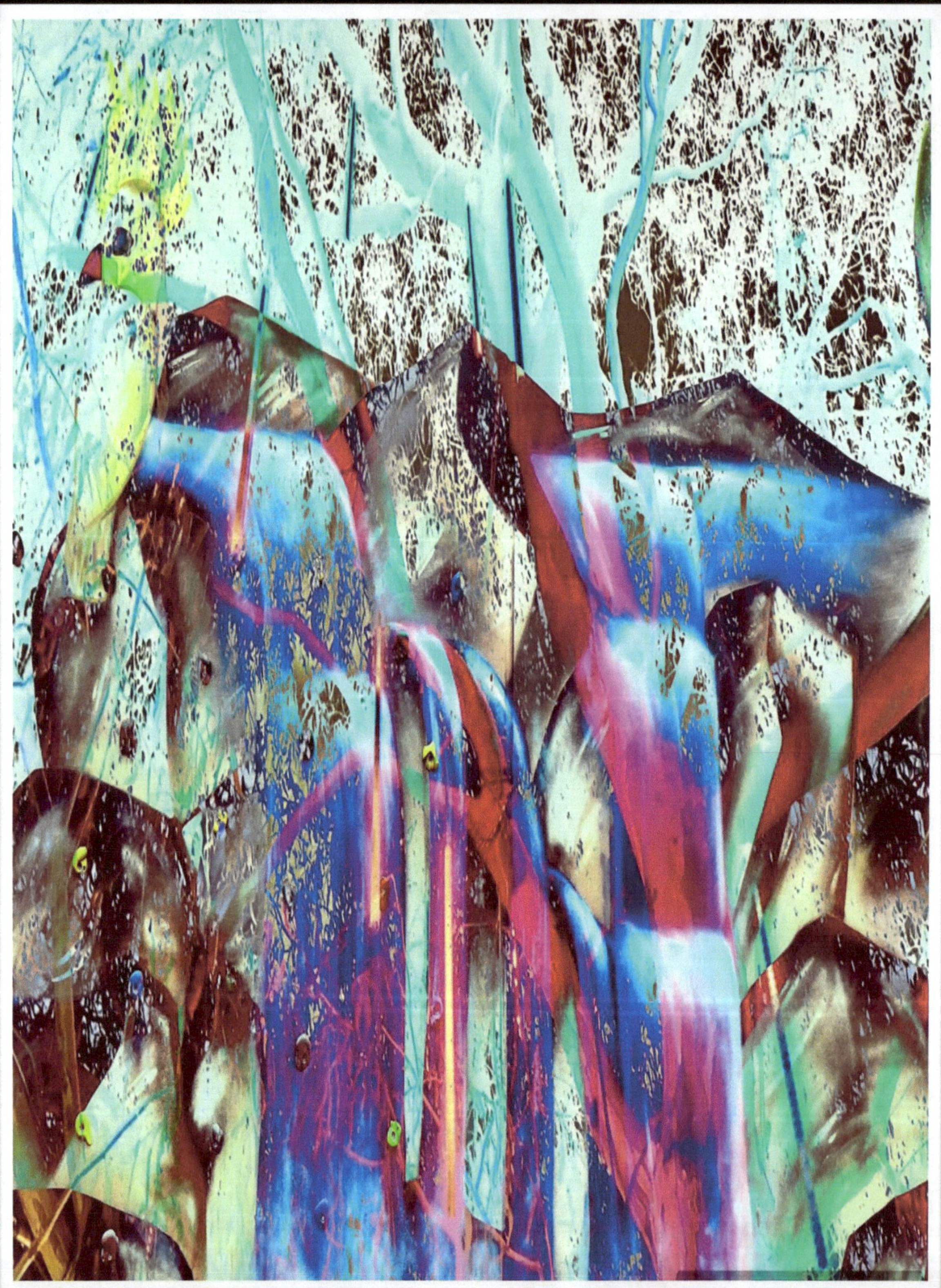

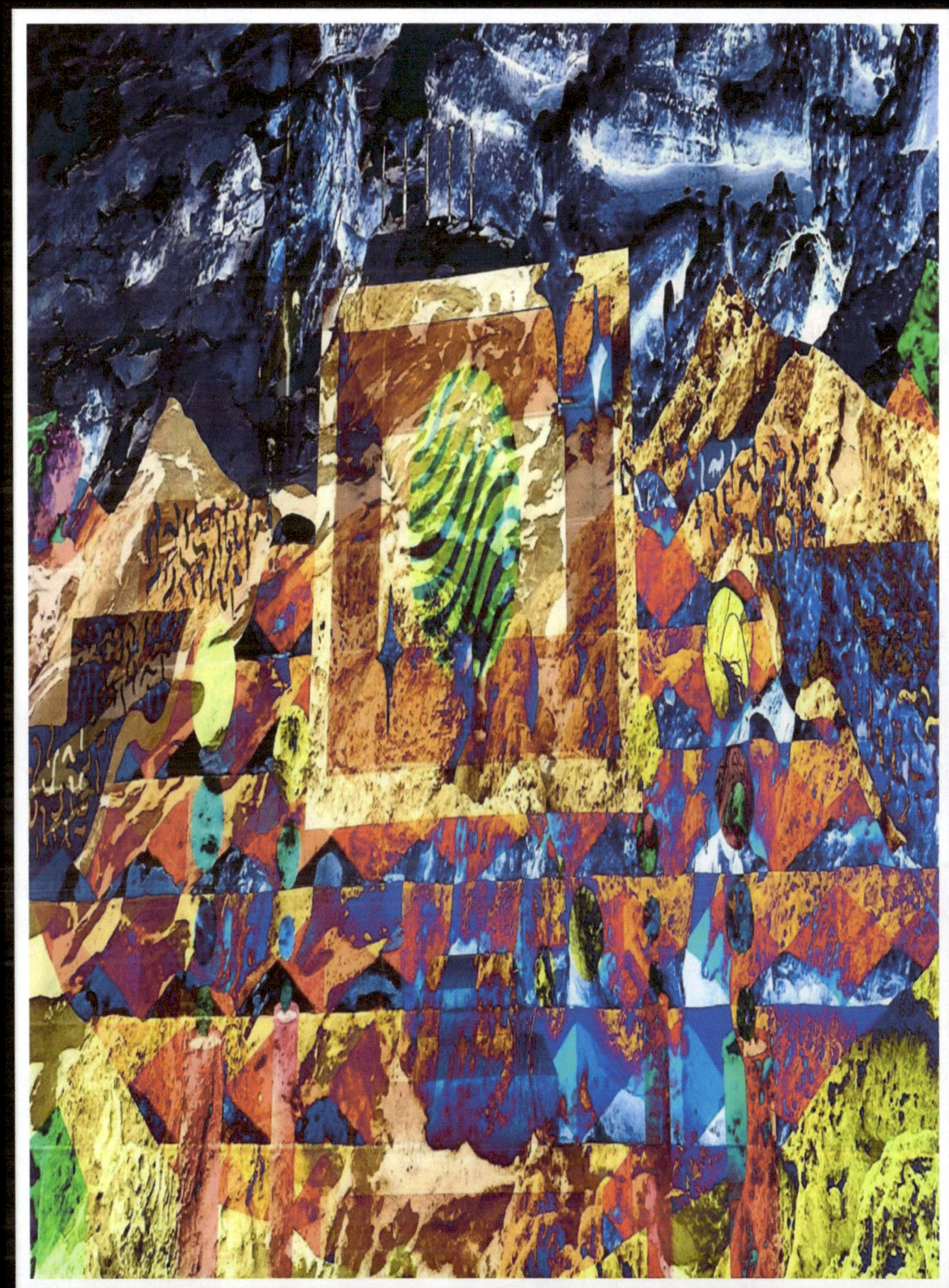

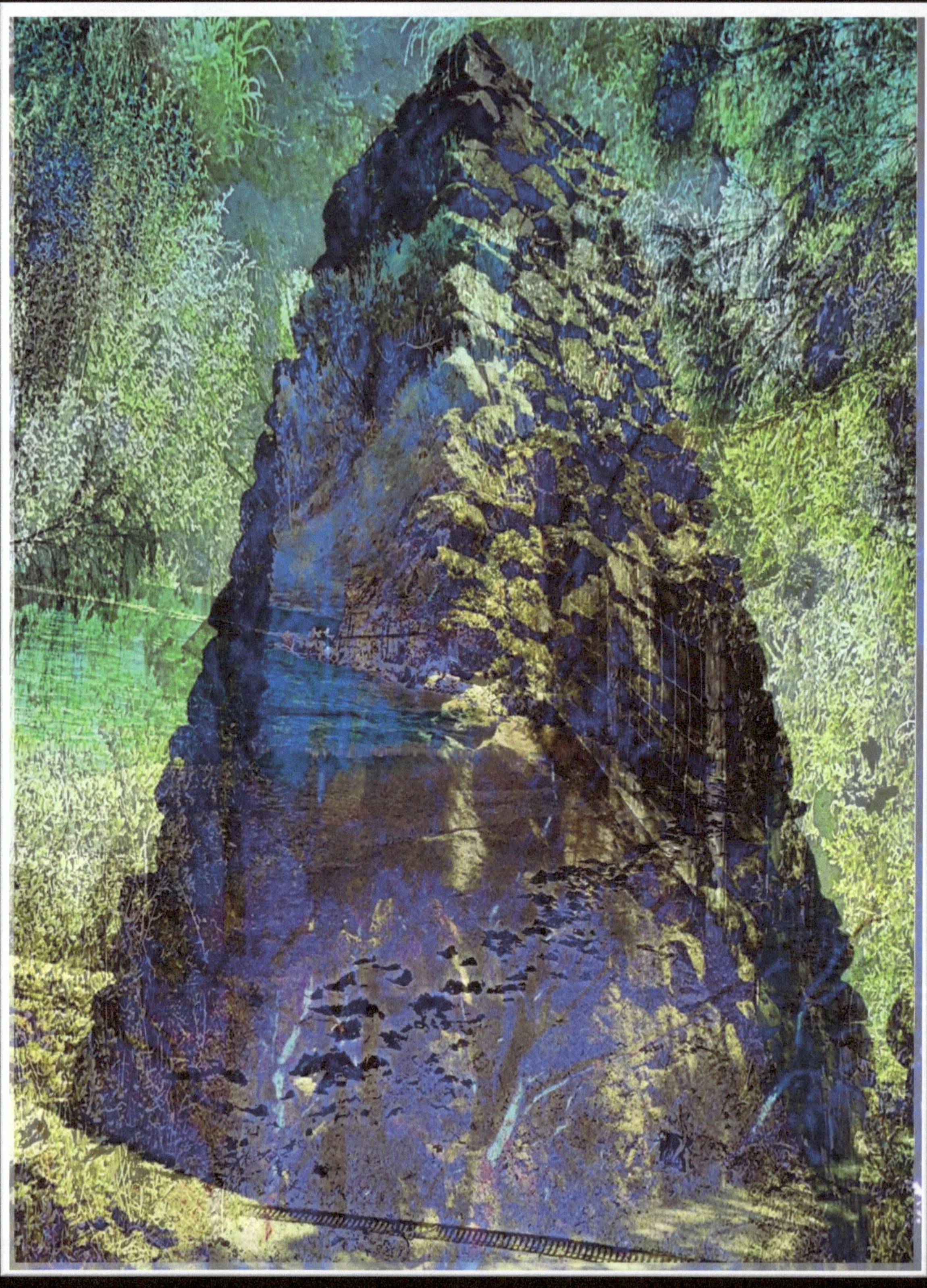

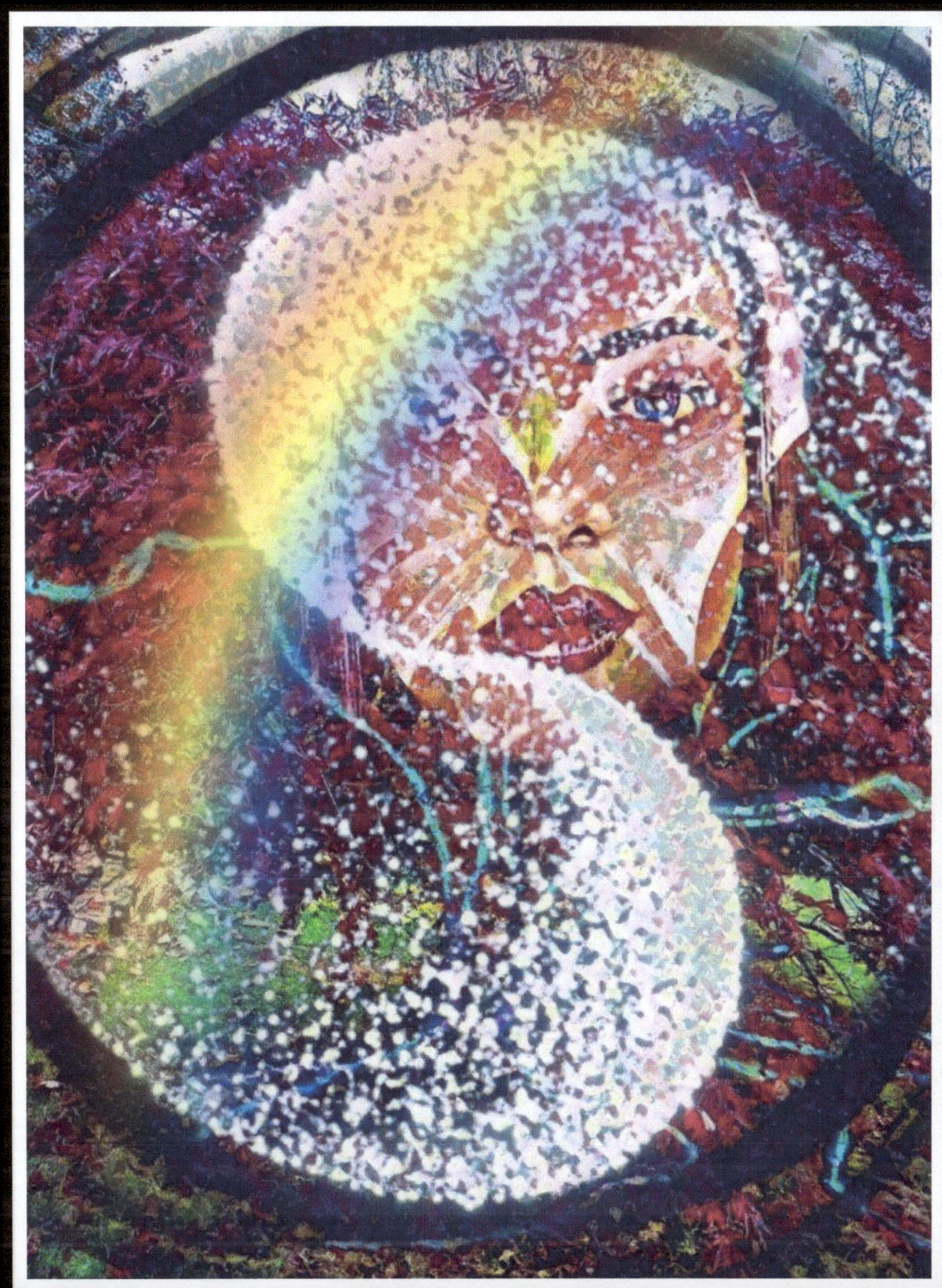

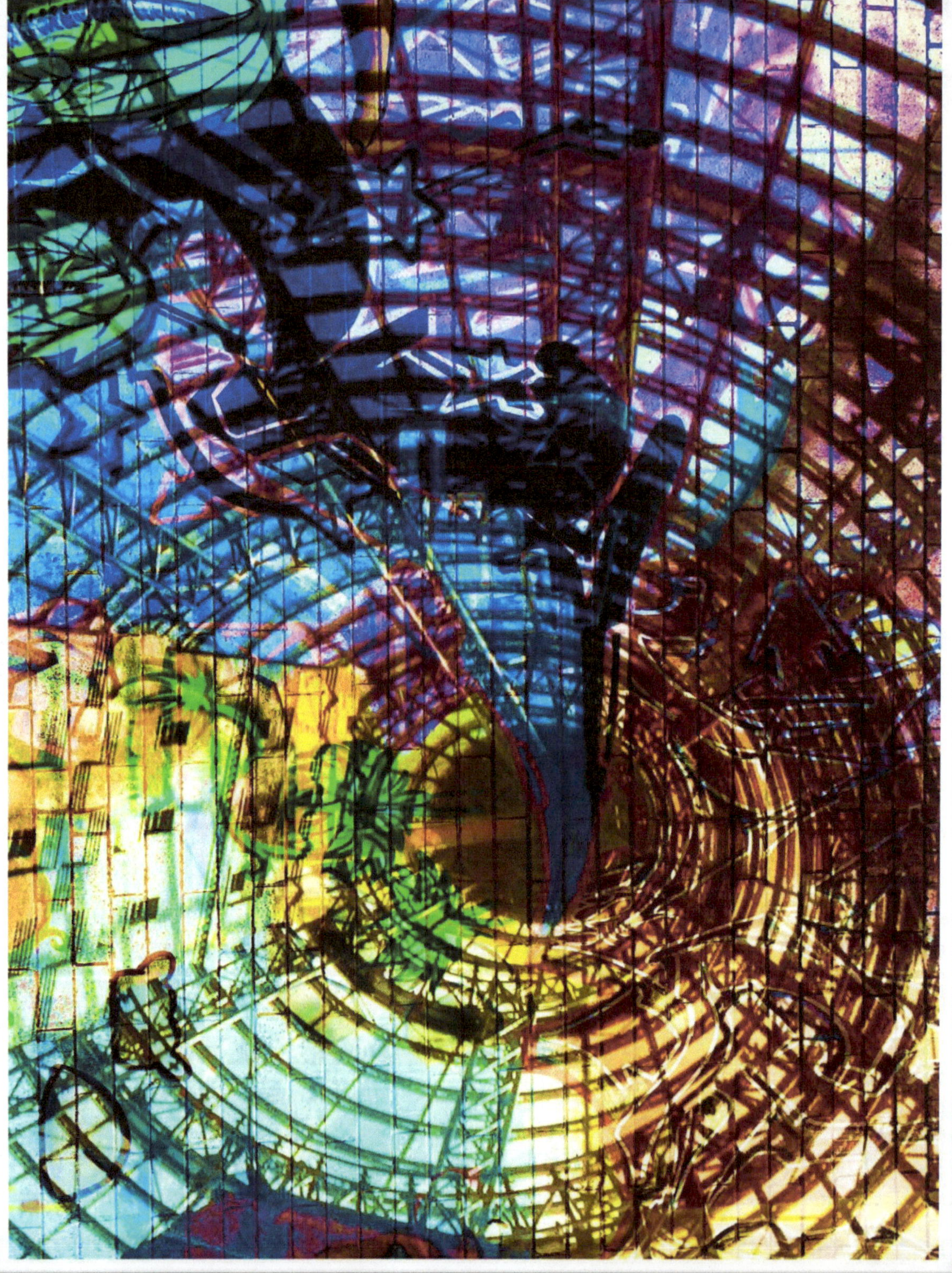

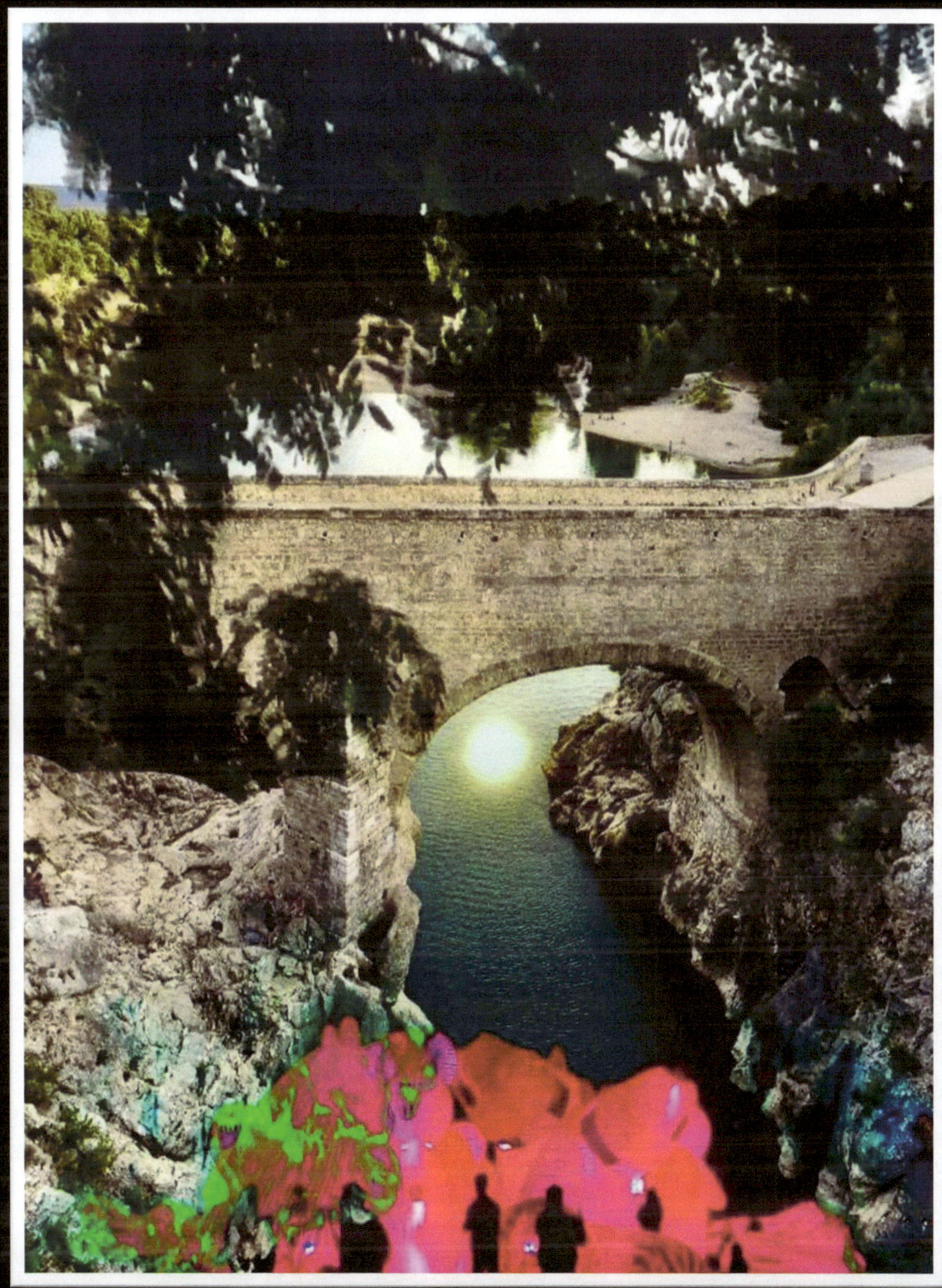

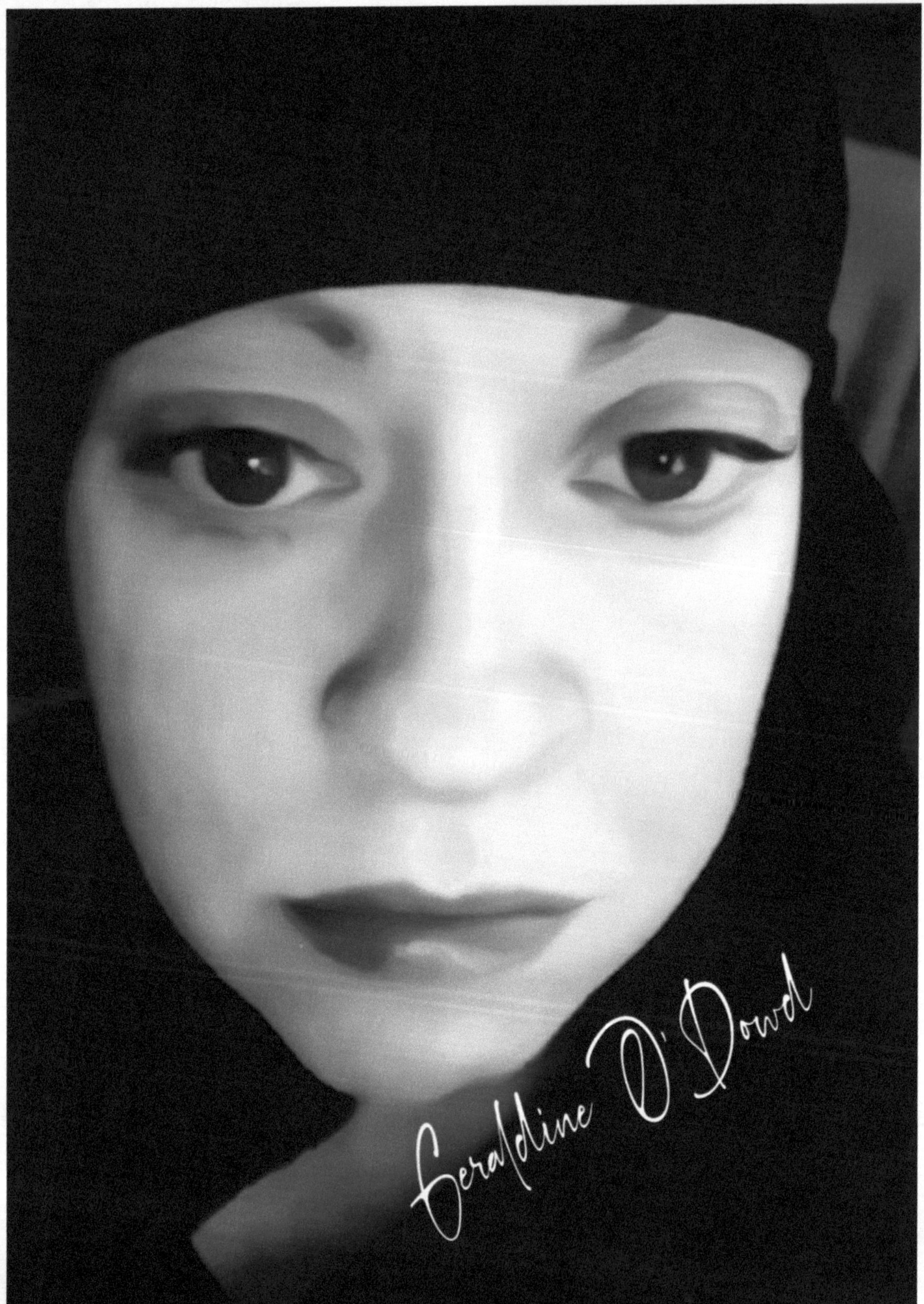
Geraldine O'Dowd

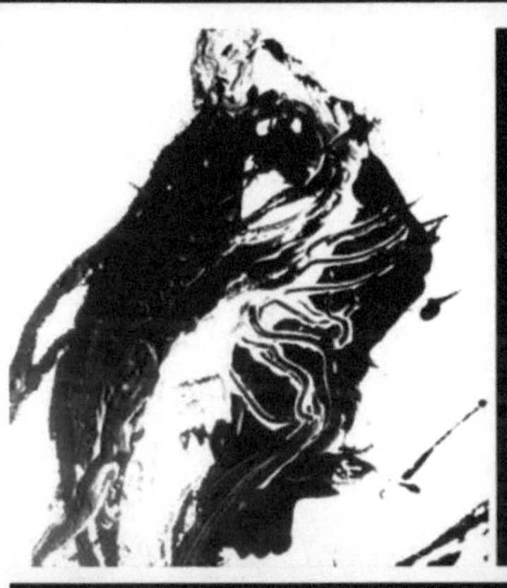 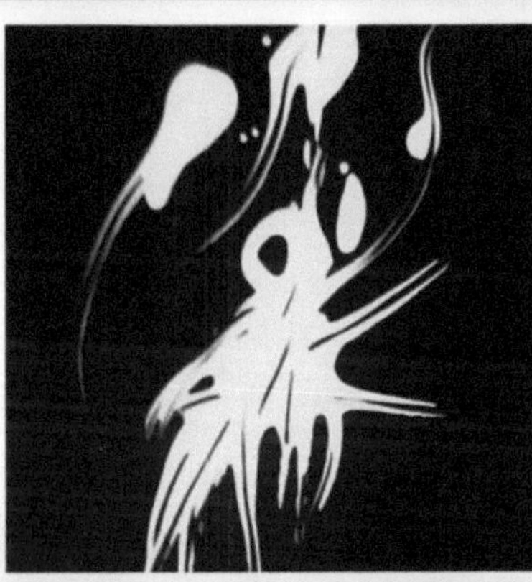 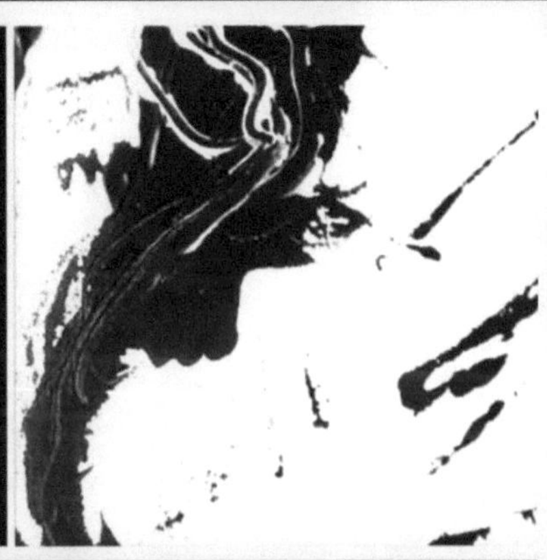

About Geraldine O'Dowd

Geraldine is a poet and artist from North Yorkshire, England. She recently released her very first publication "Insomnia Woman." It is a must have collection of poetry and that portrays her life story. She hopes to shed light on domestic abuse through her poetic truths.

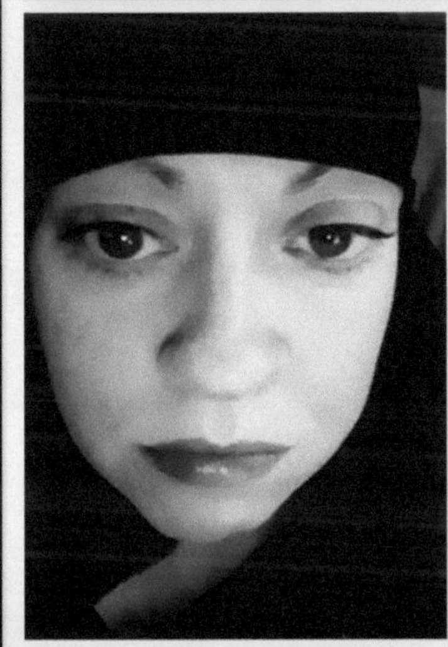 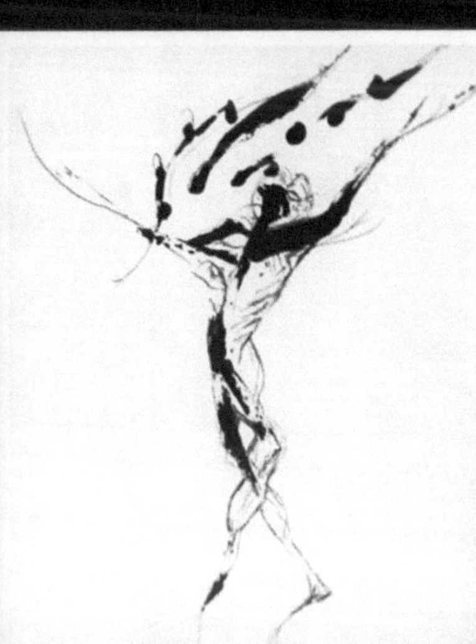 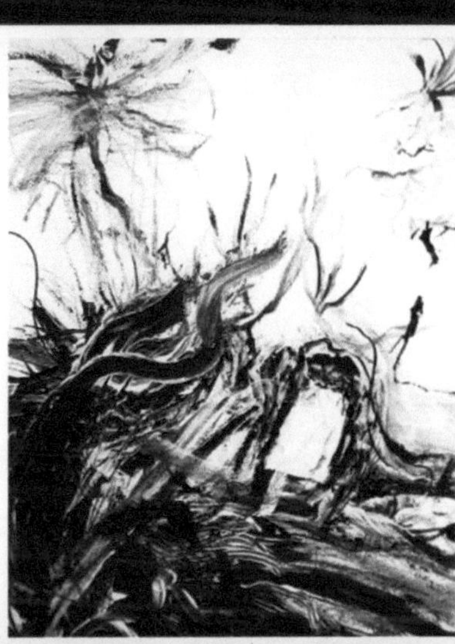

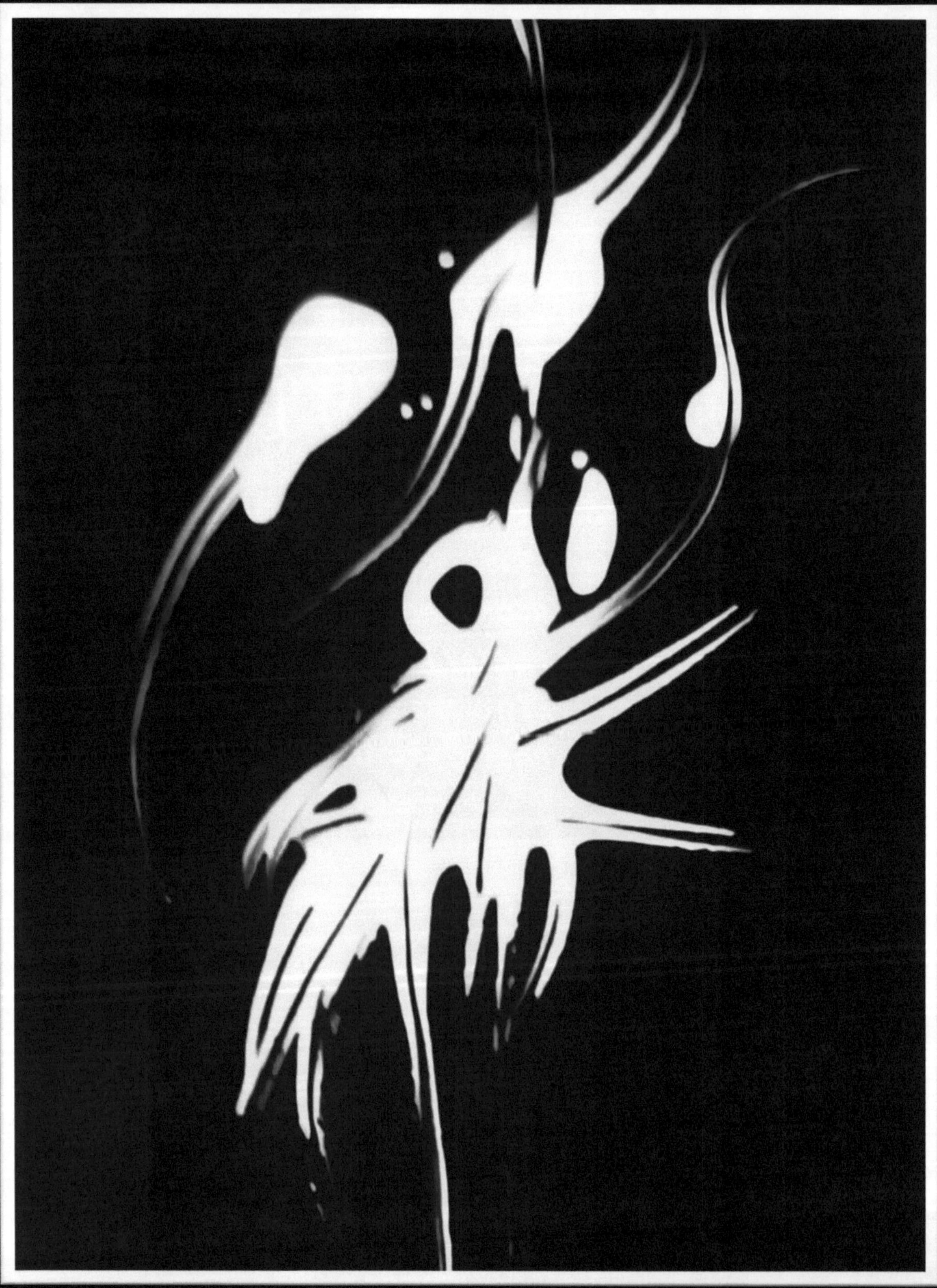

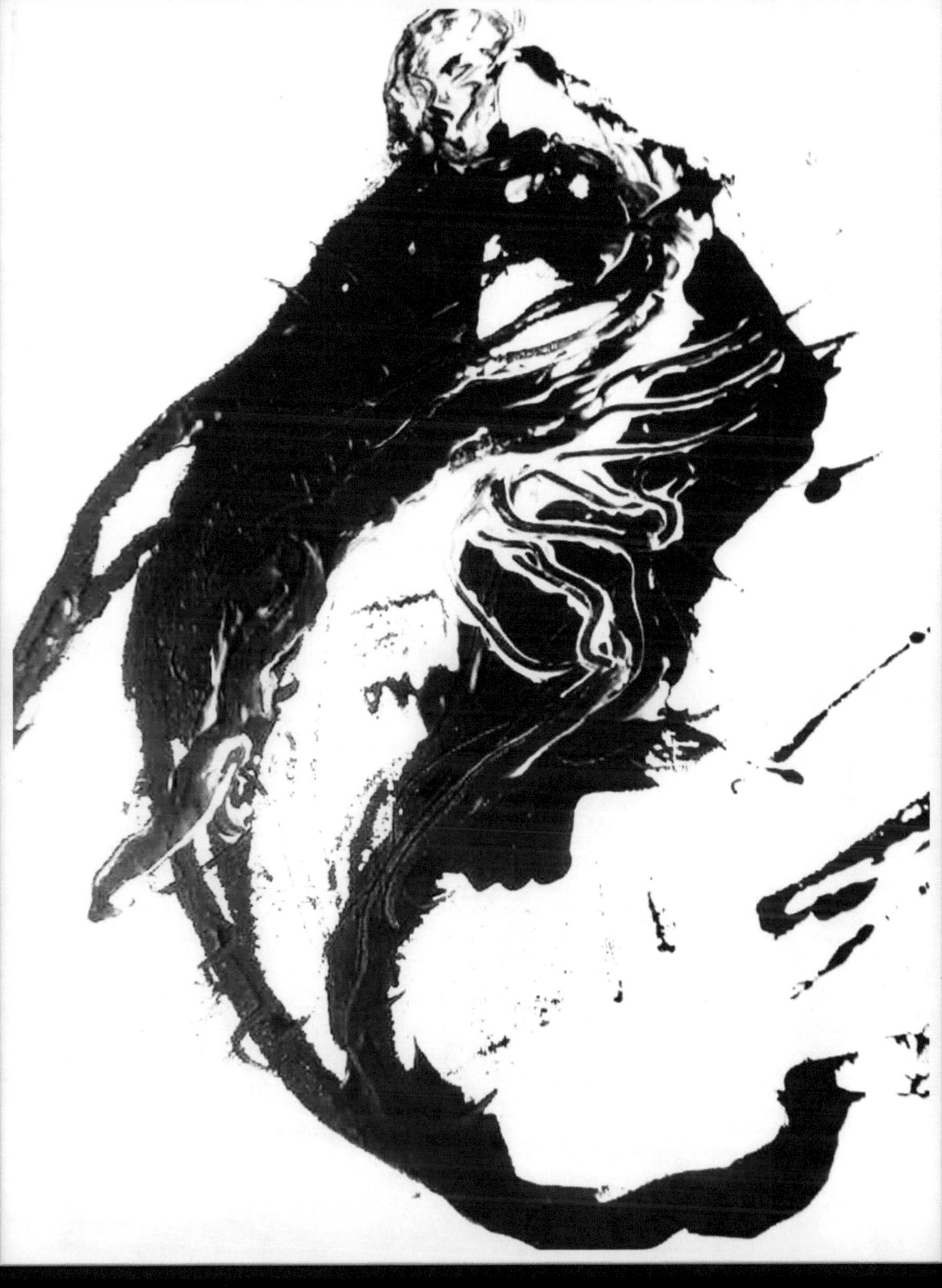

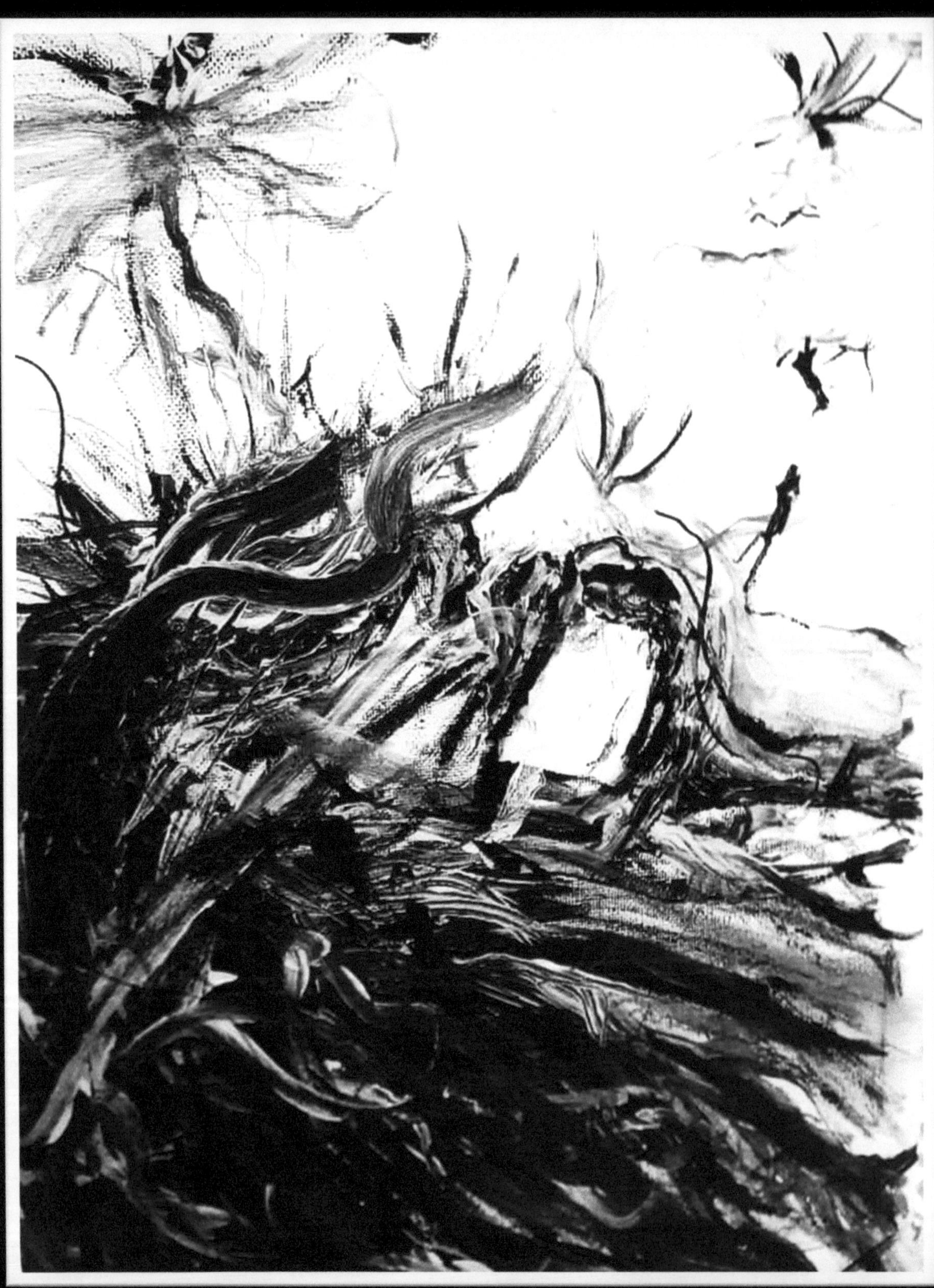

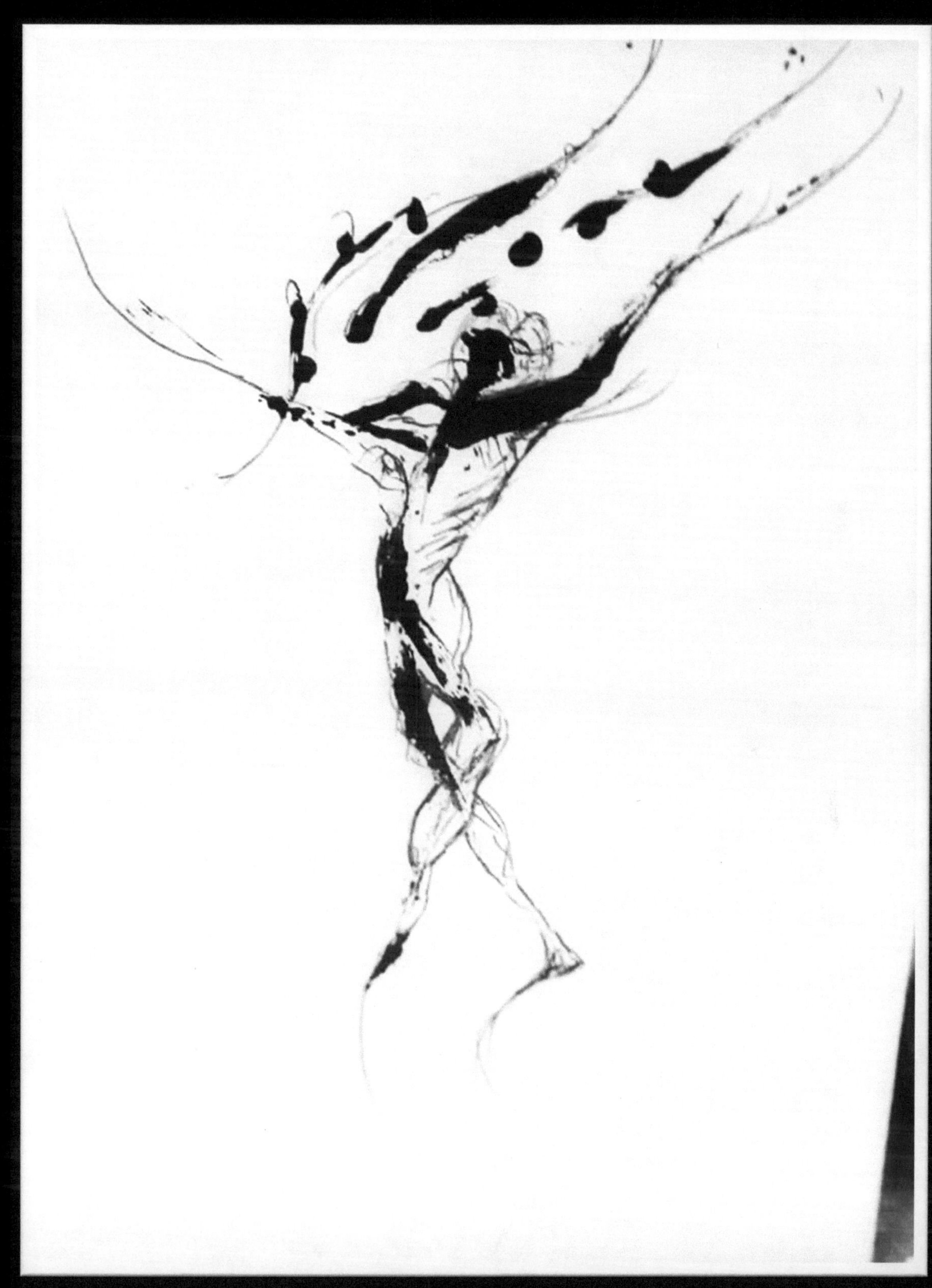

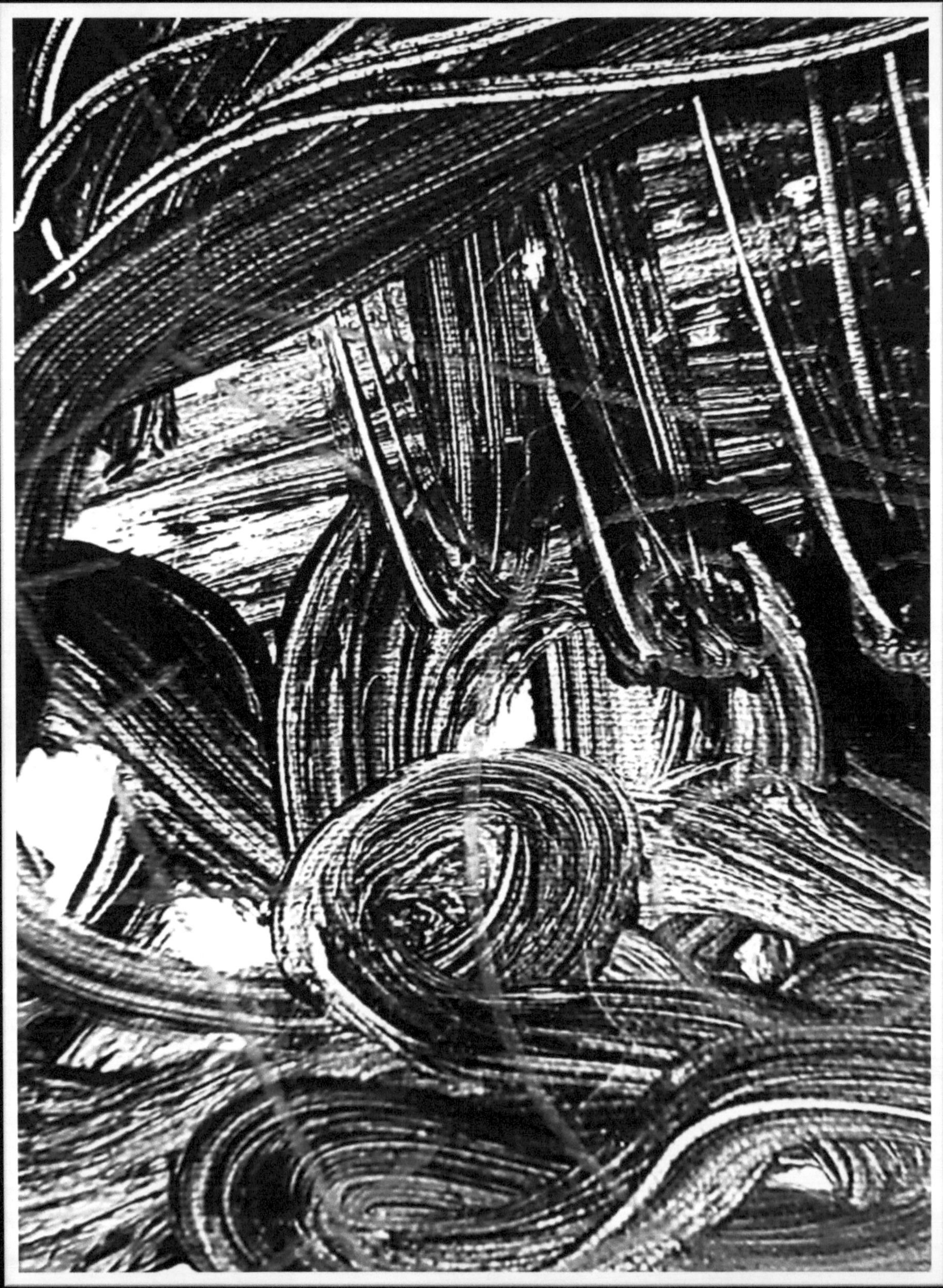

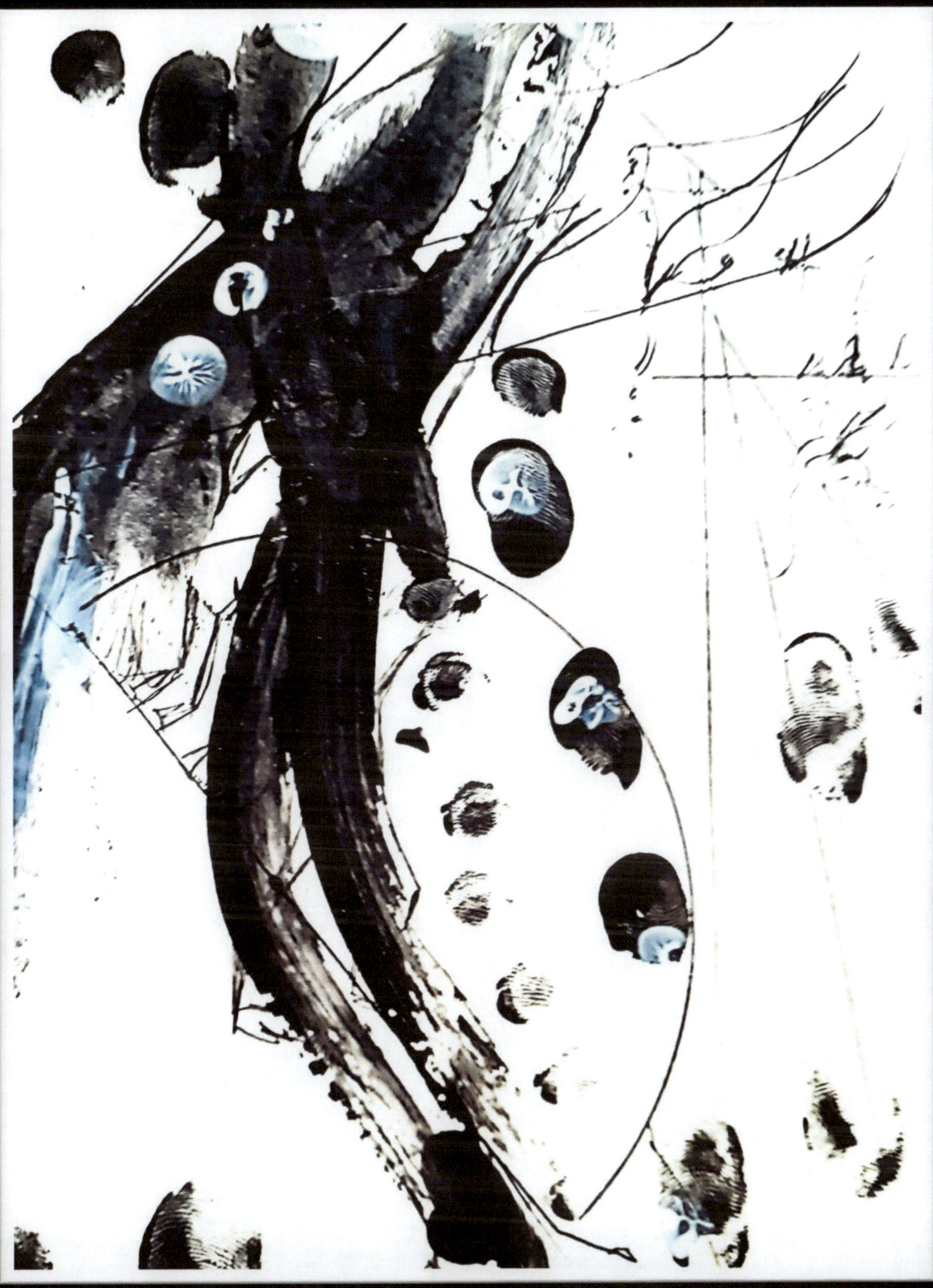

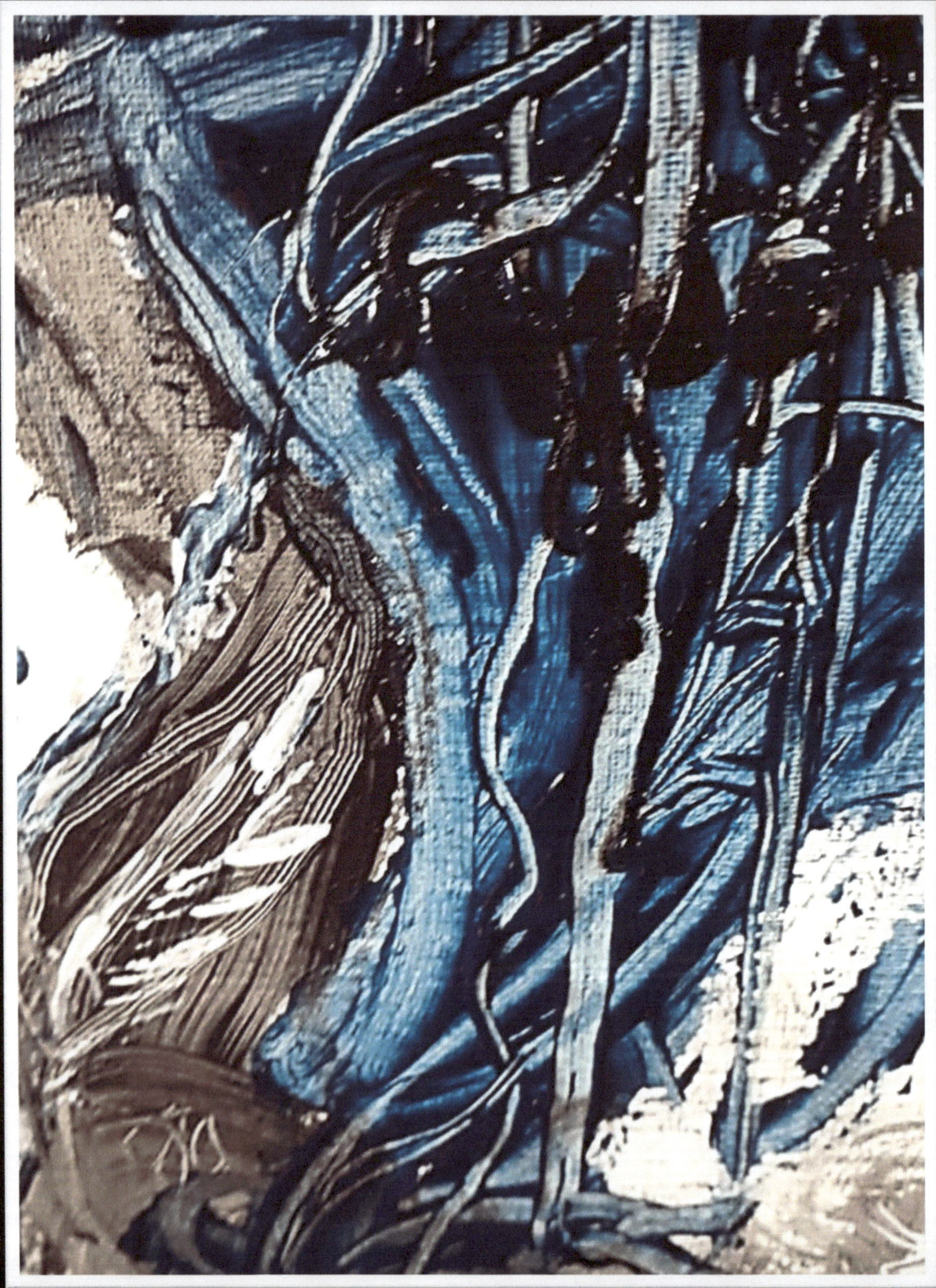

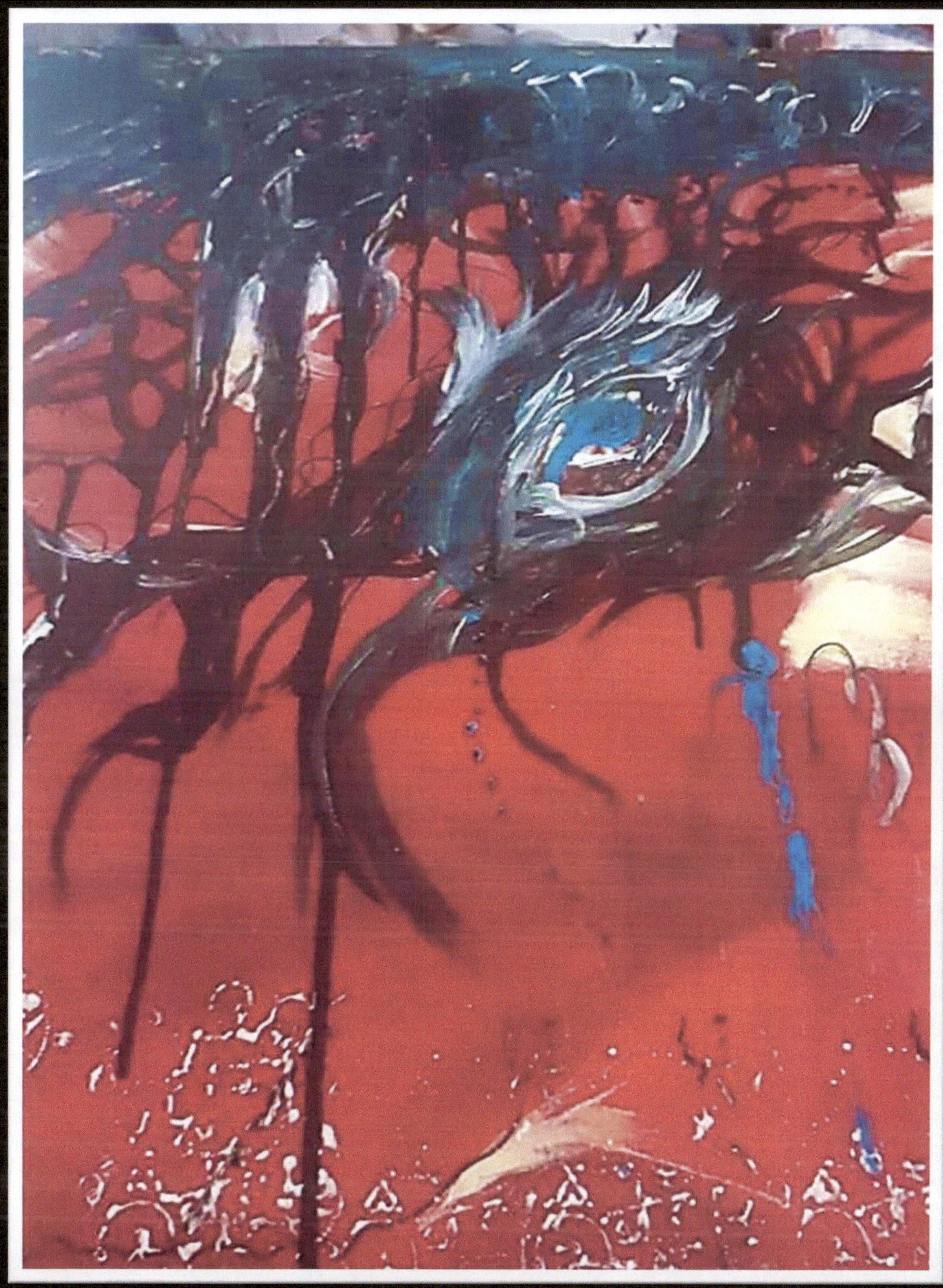

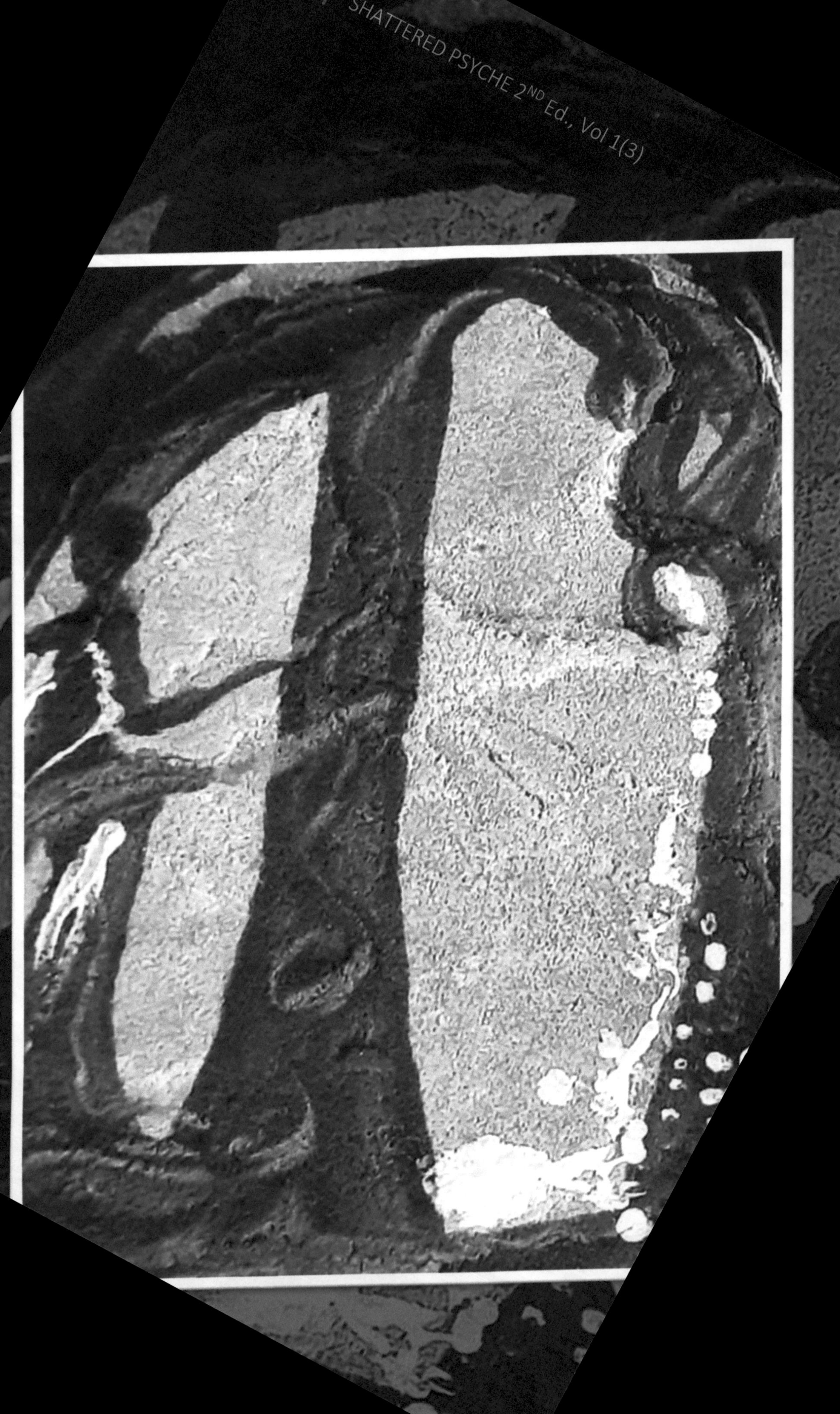

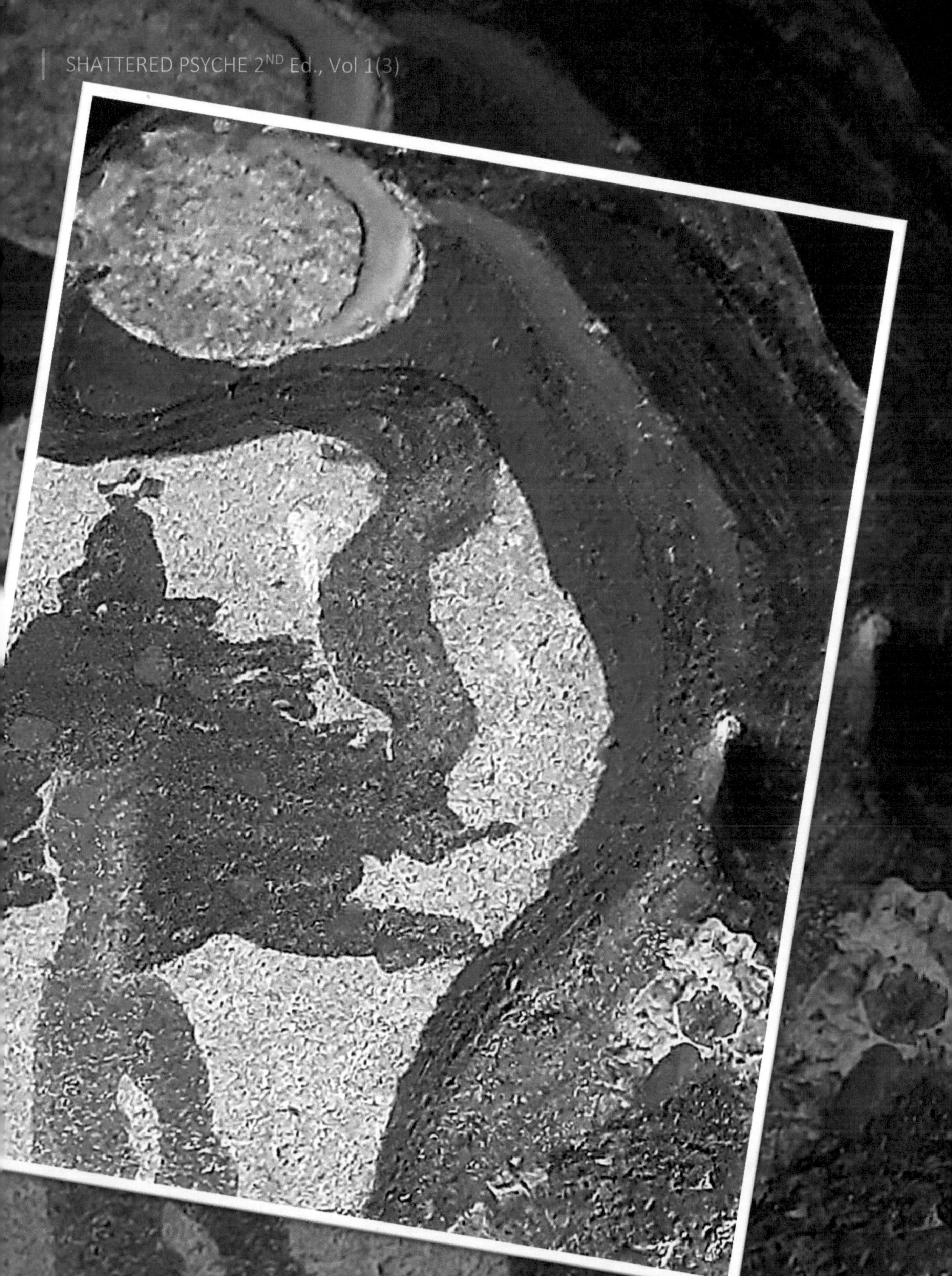

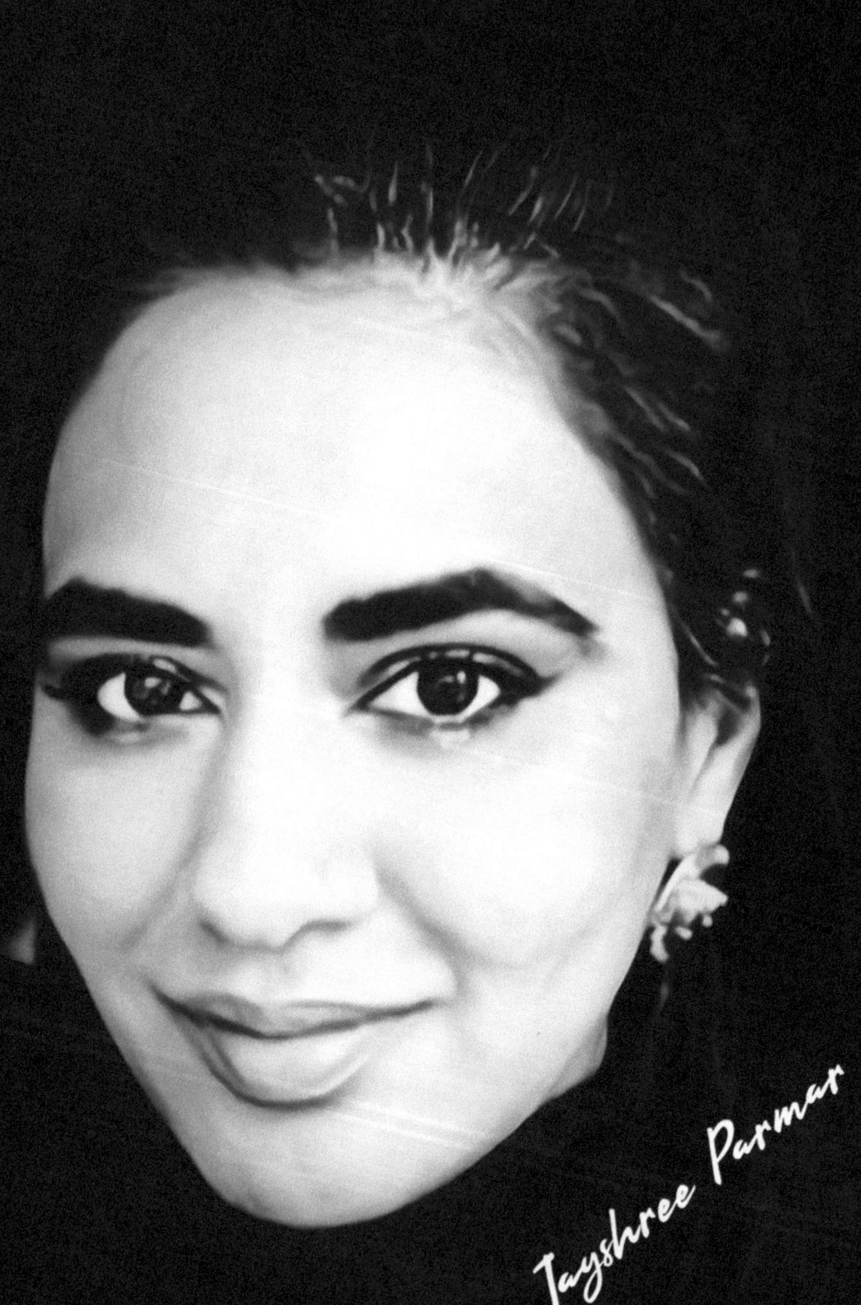
Jayshree Parmar

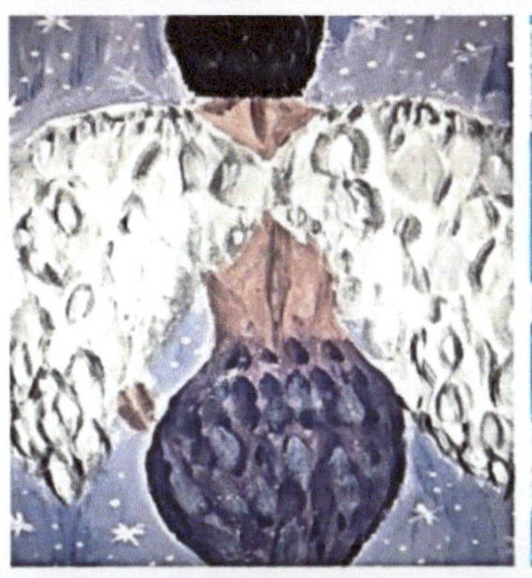
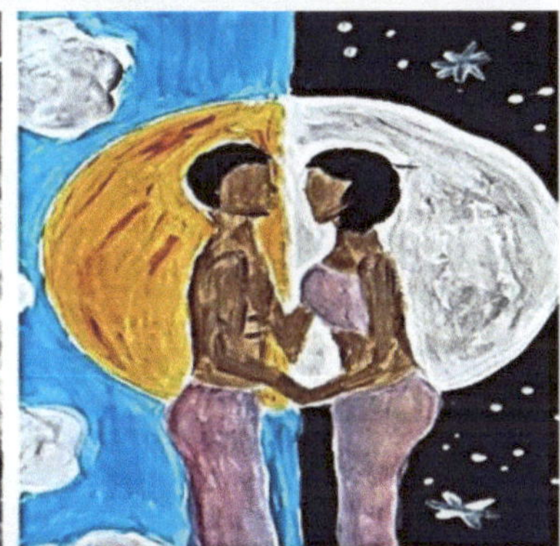
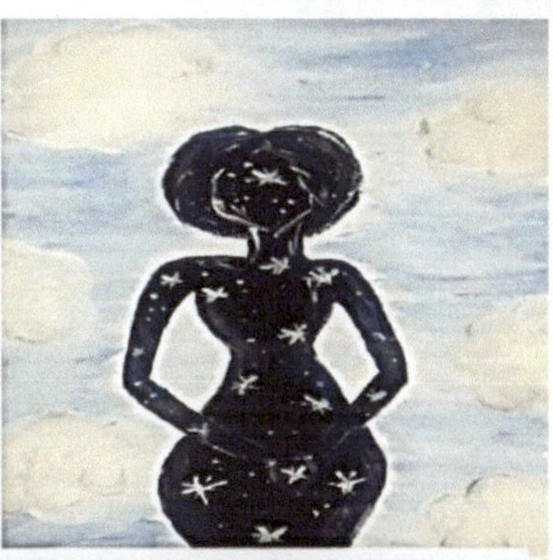

About Jayshree Parmar

Jayshree is a HR professional by day and dreamer by night. Books and words have always been a love affair and being transported into another world is something she loves.Following her love of books, she decided to use her creativity and imagination to create masterpieces. From poems to blog, sharing her insights to the world.

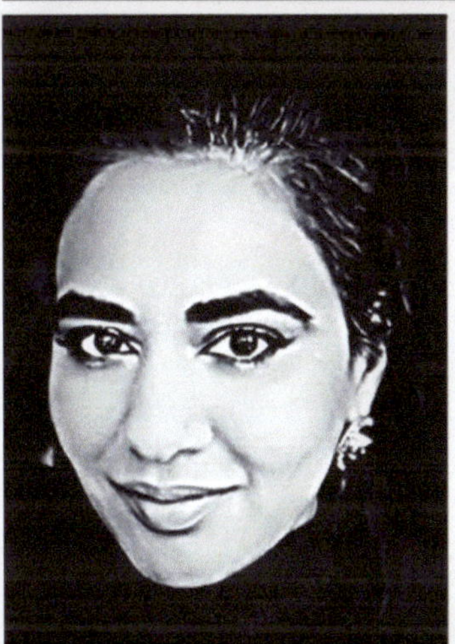
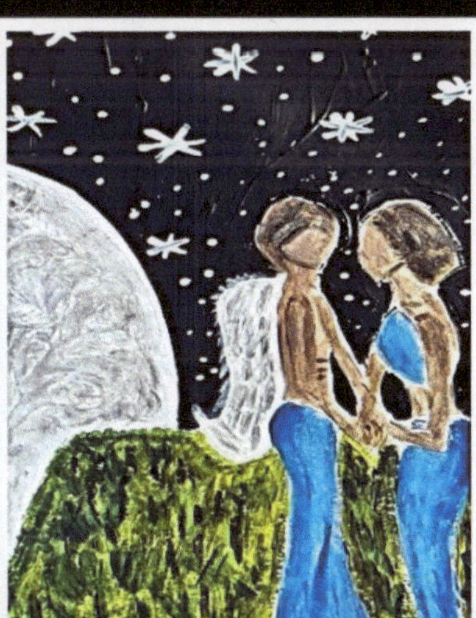
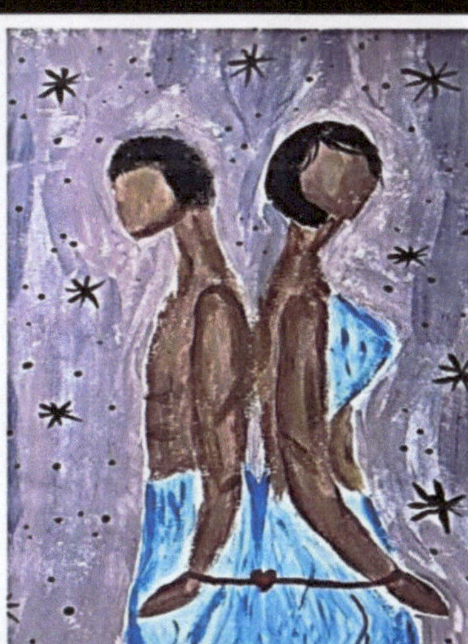

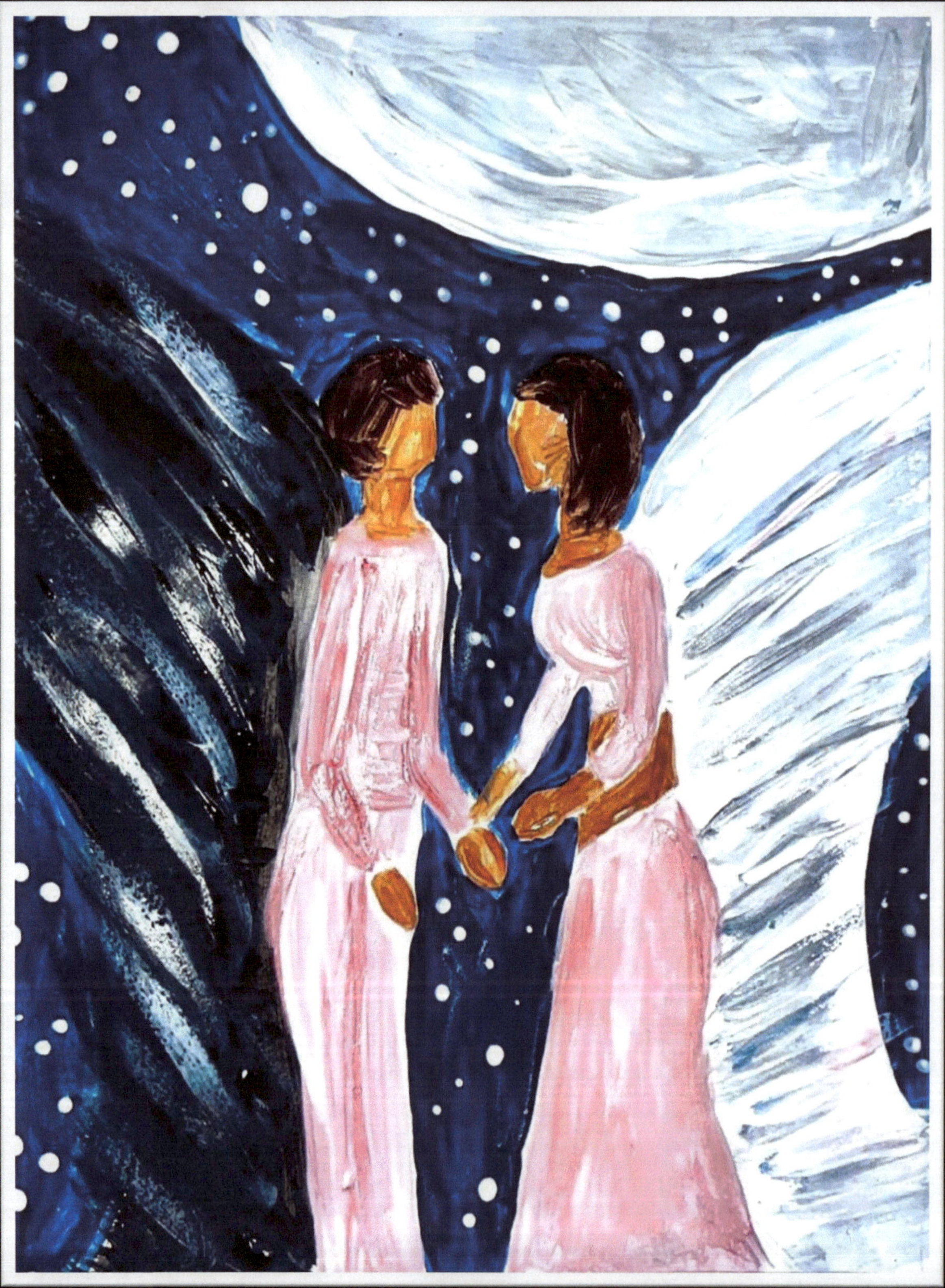

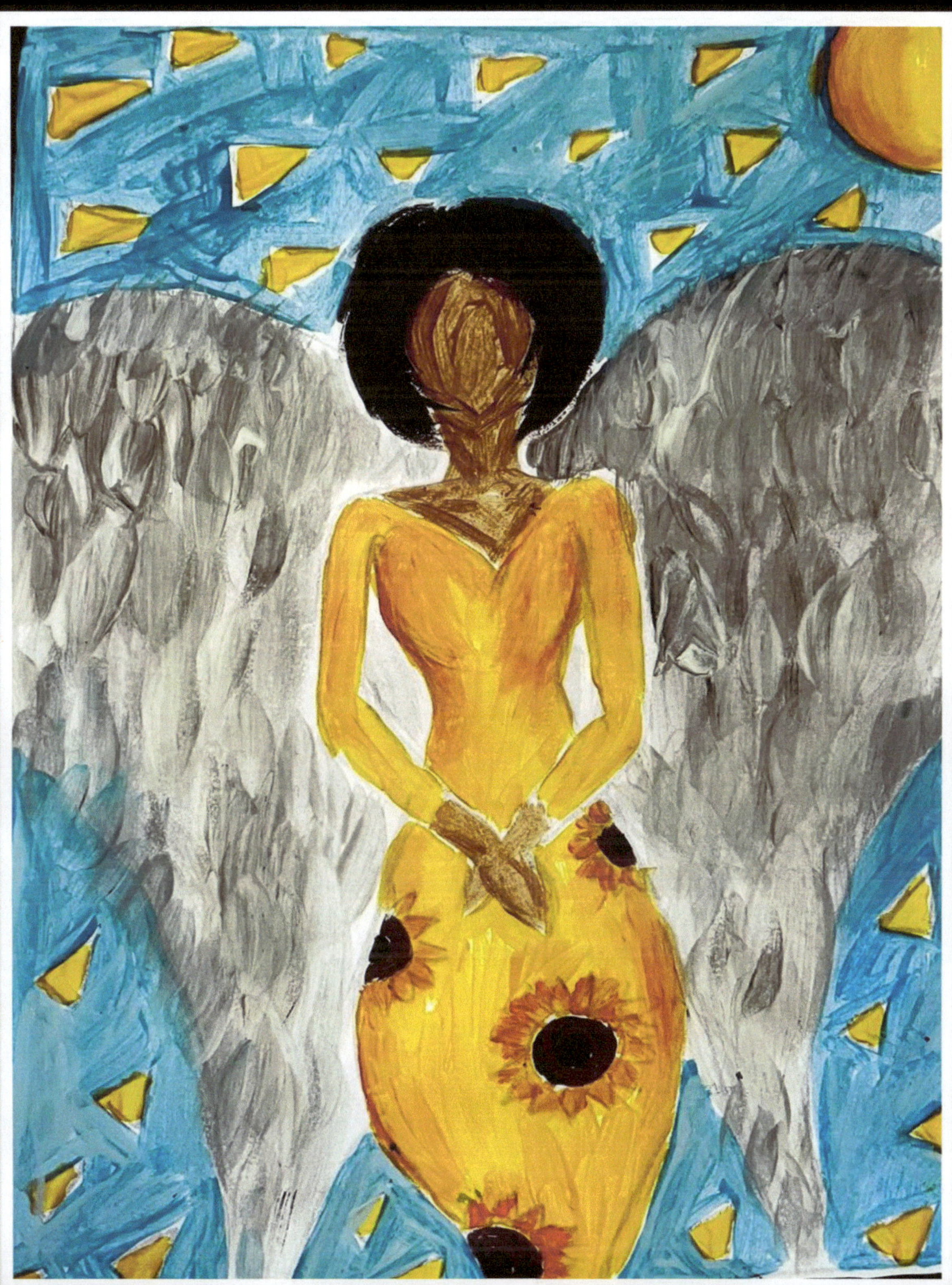

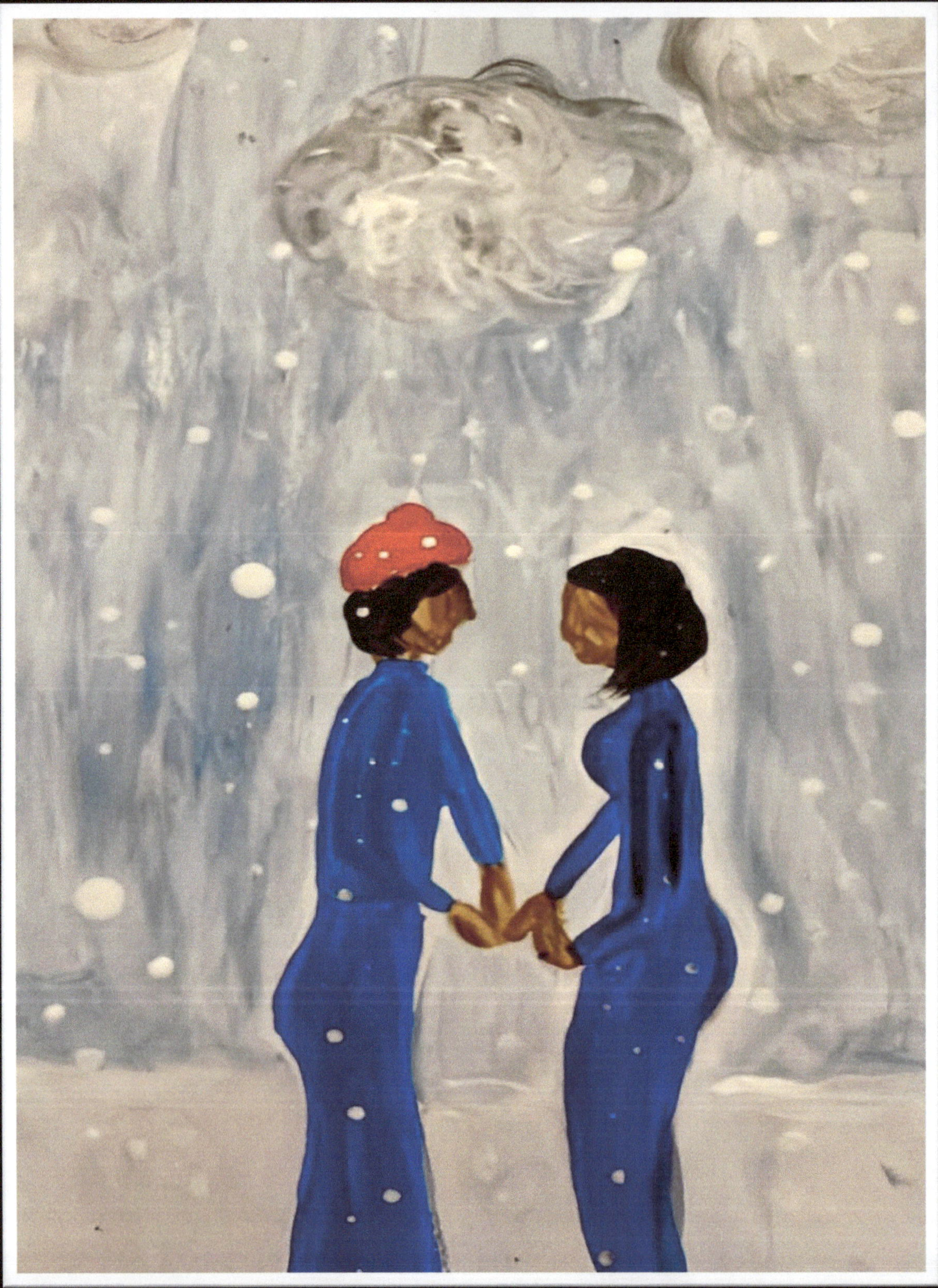

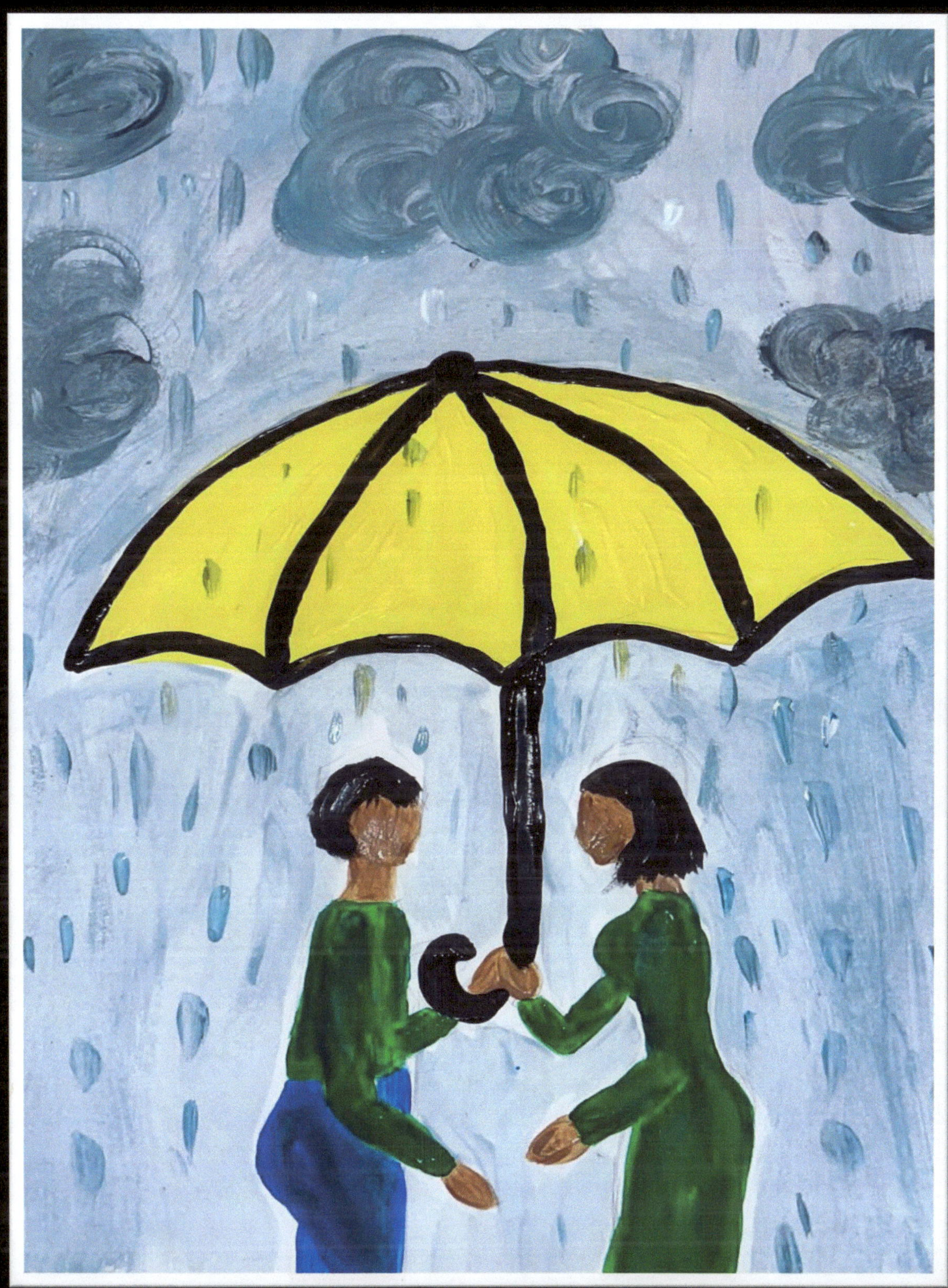

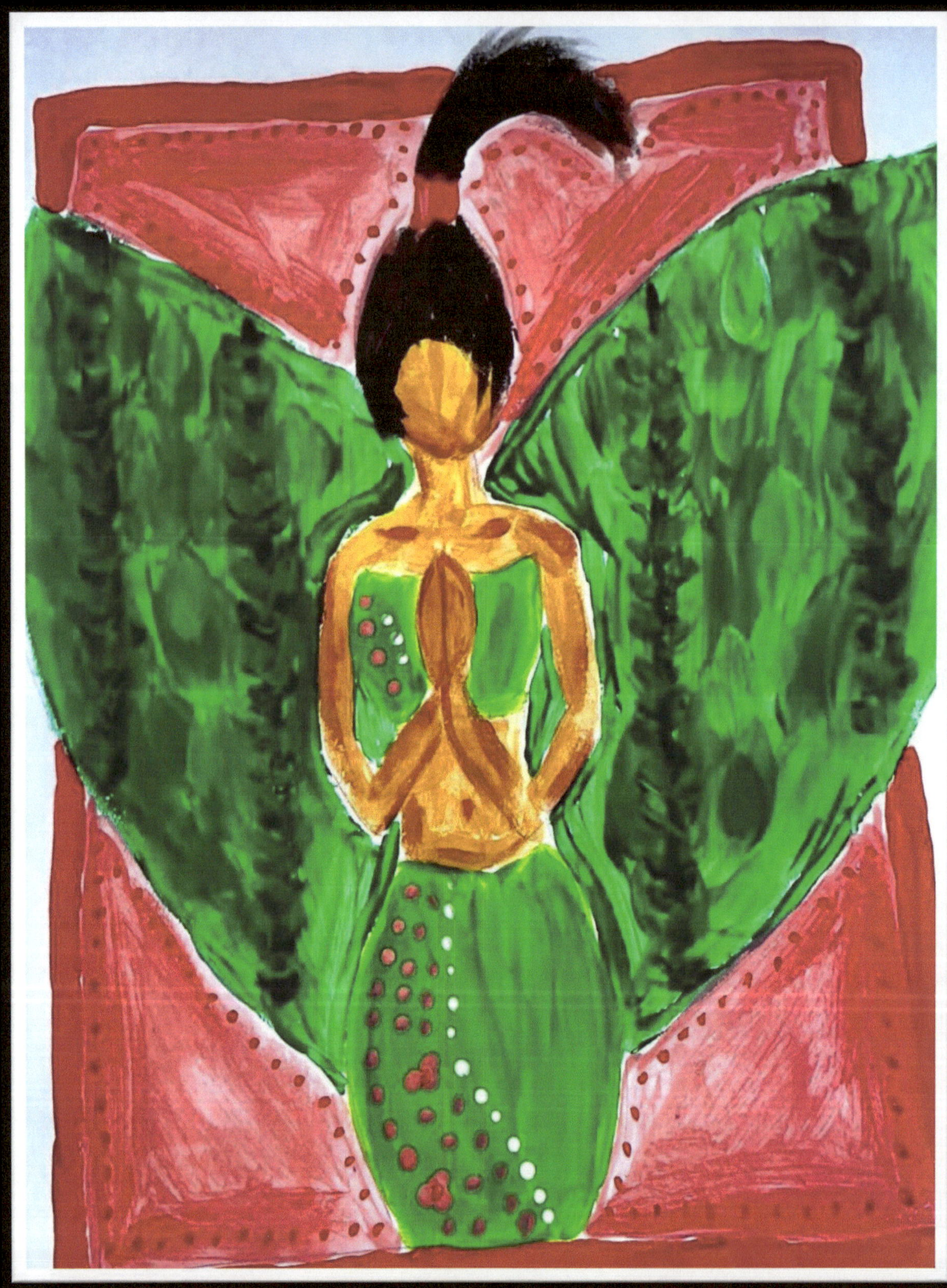

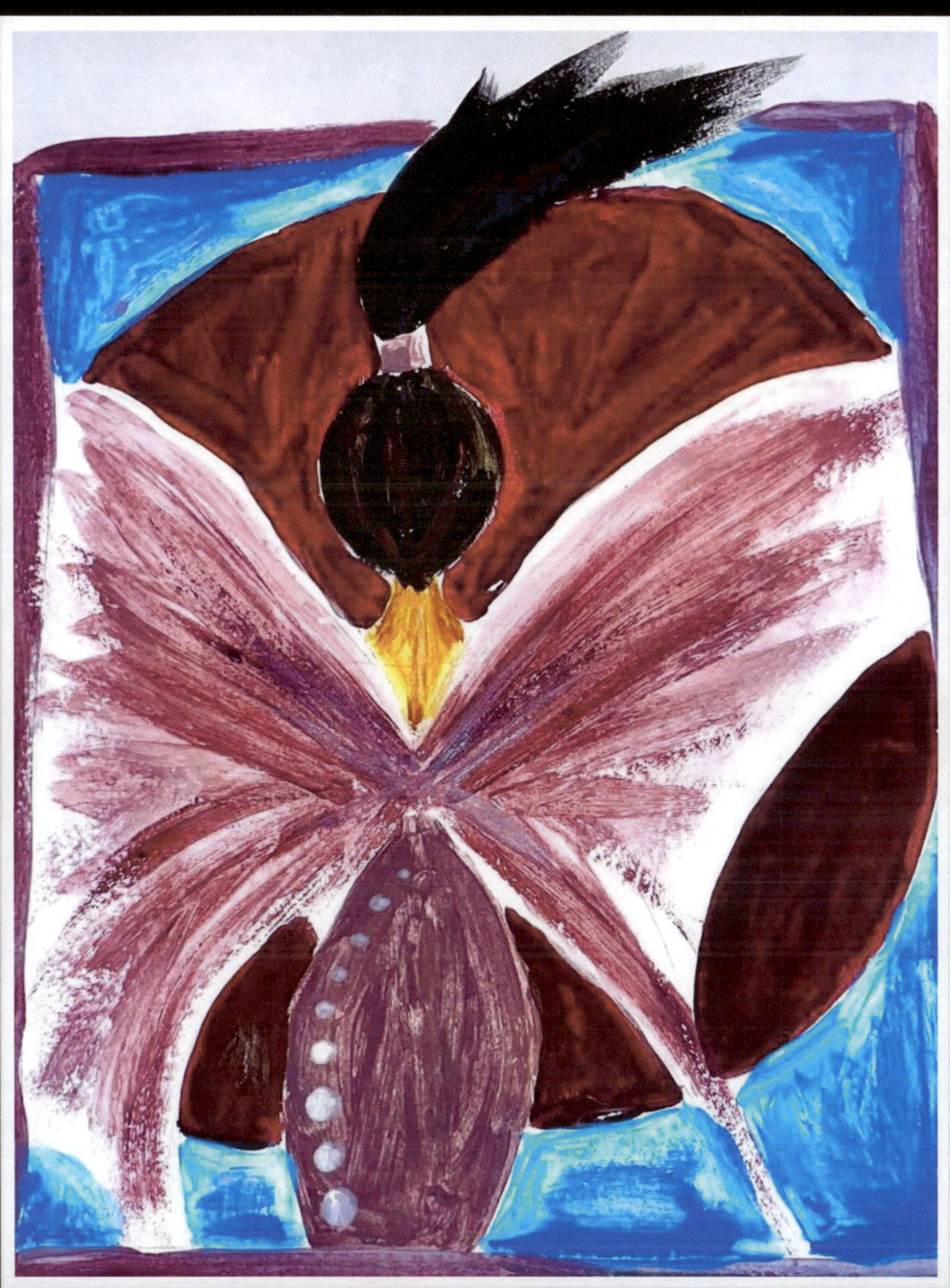

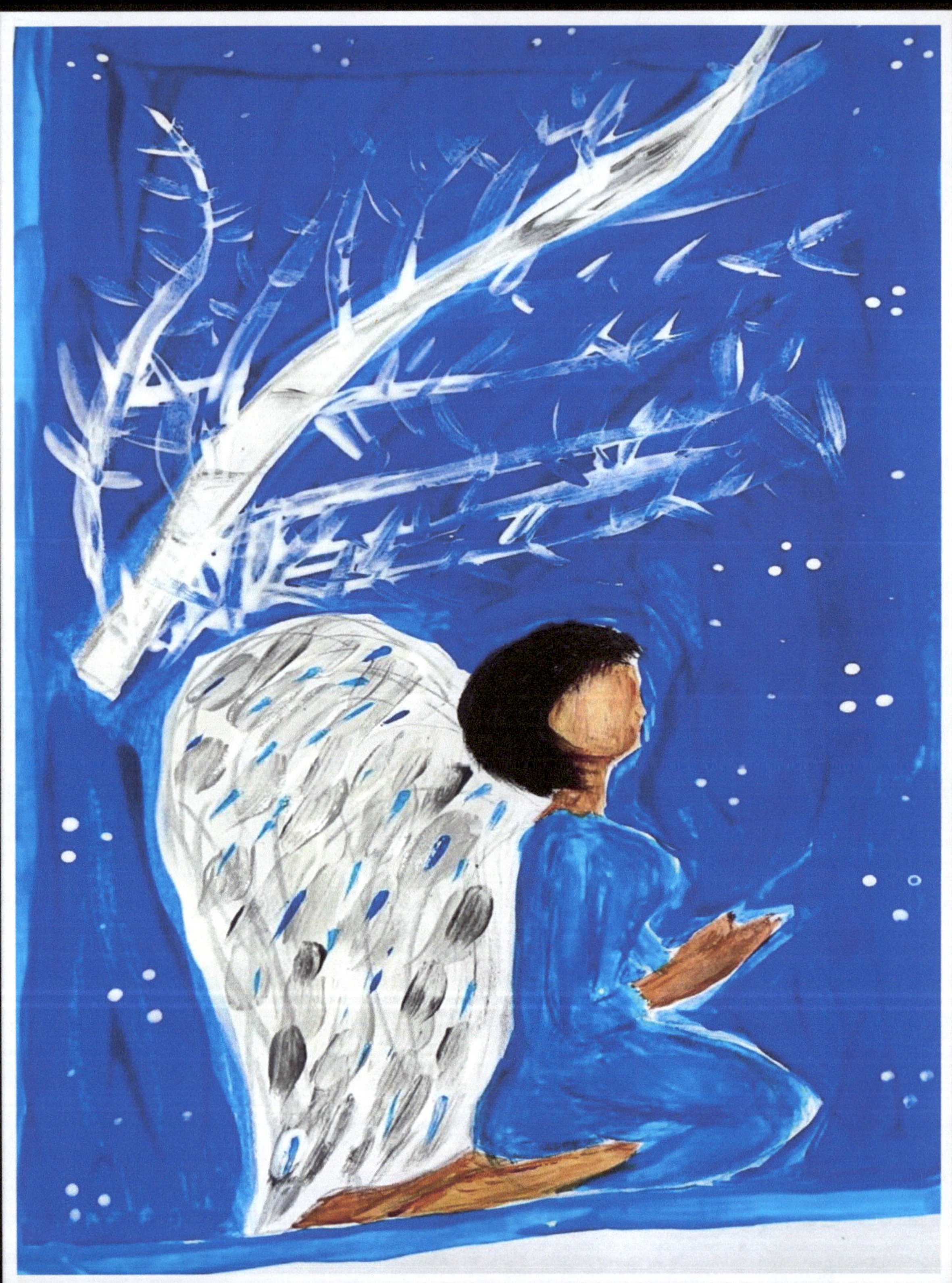

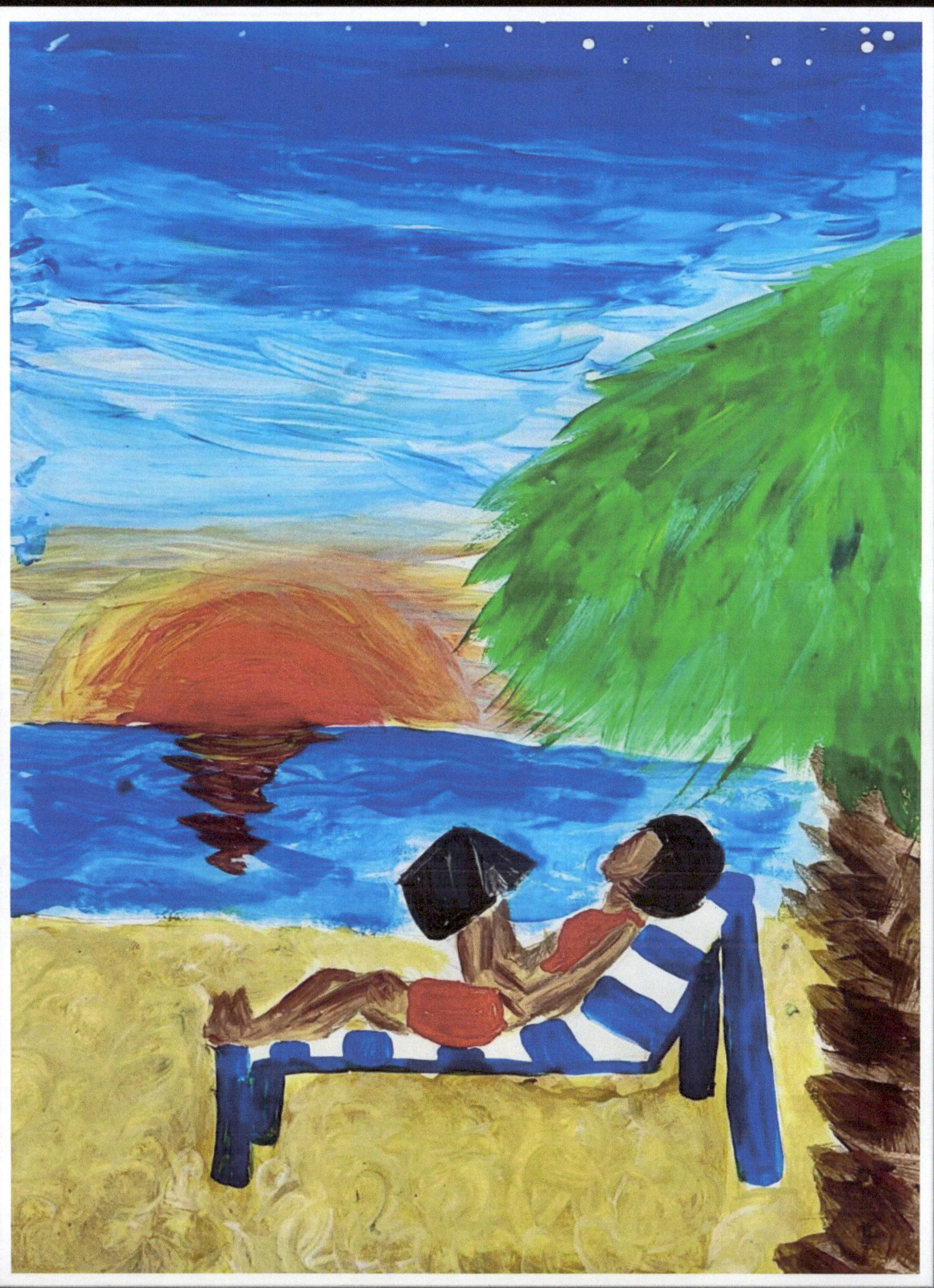

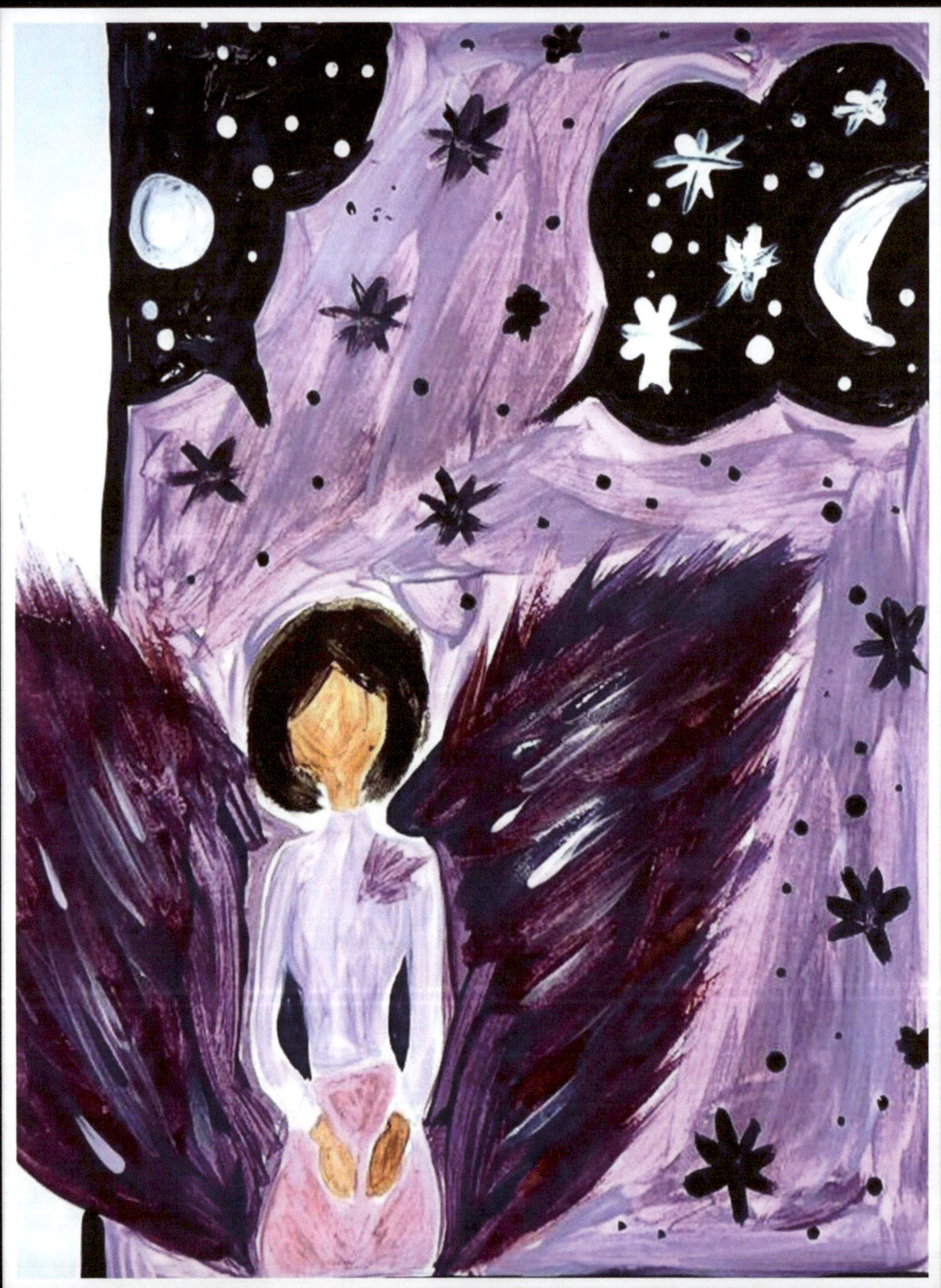

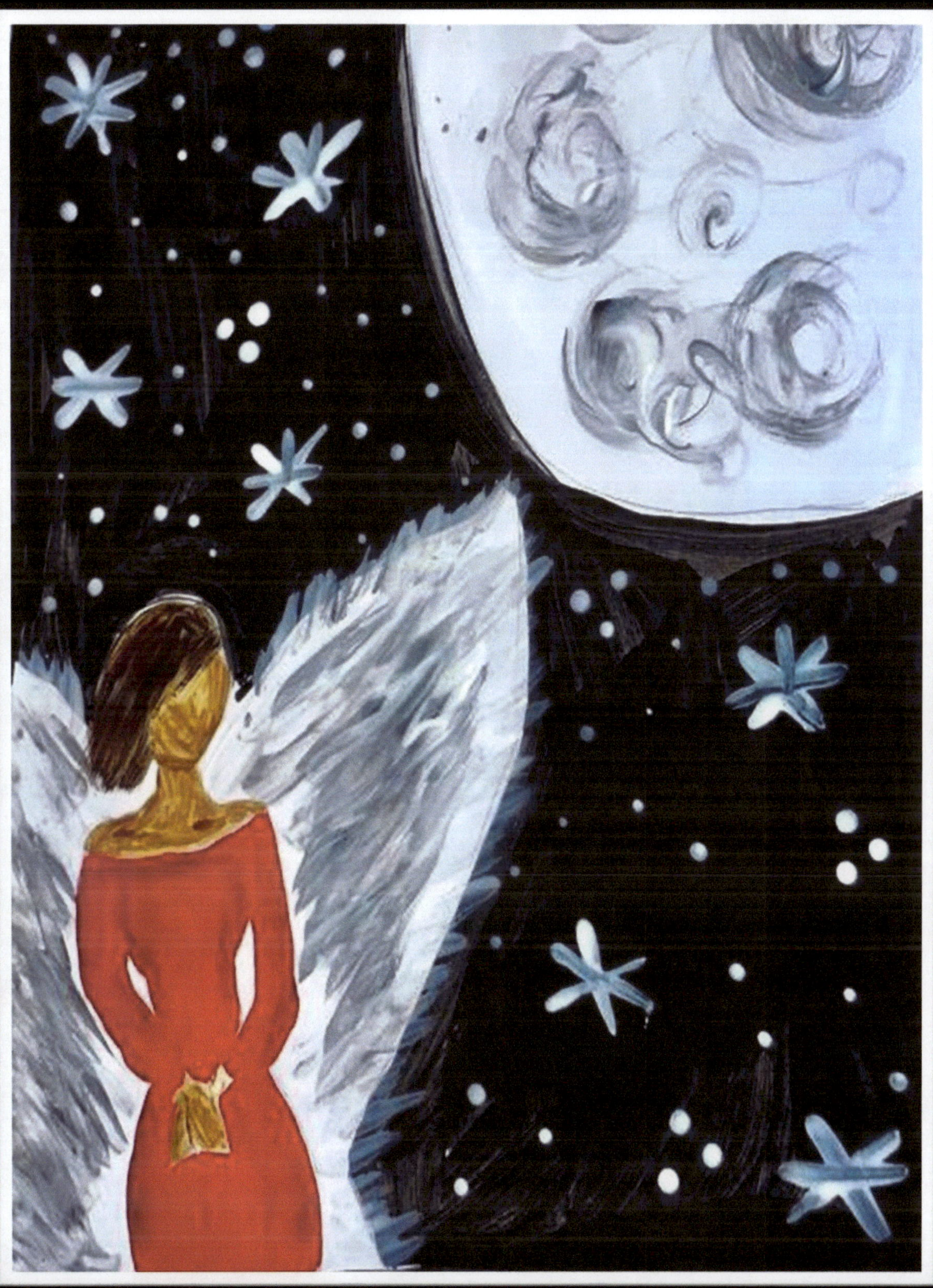

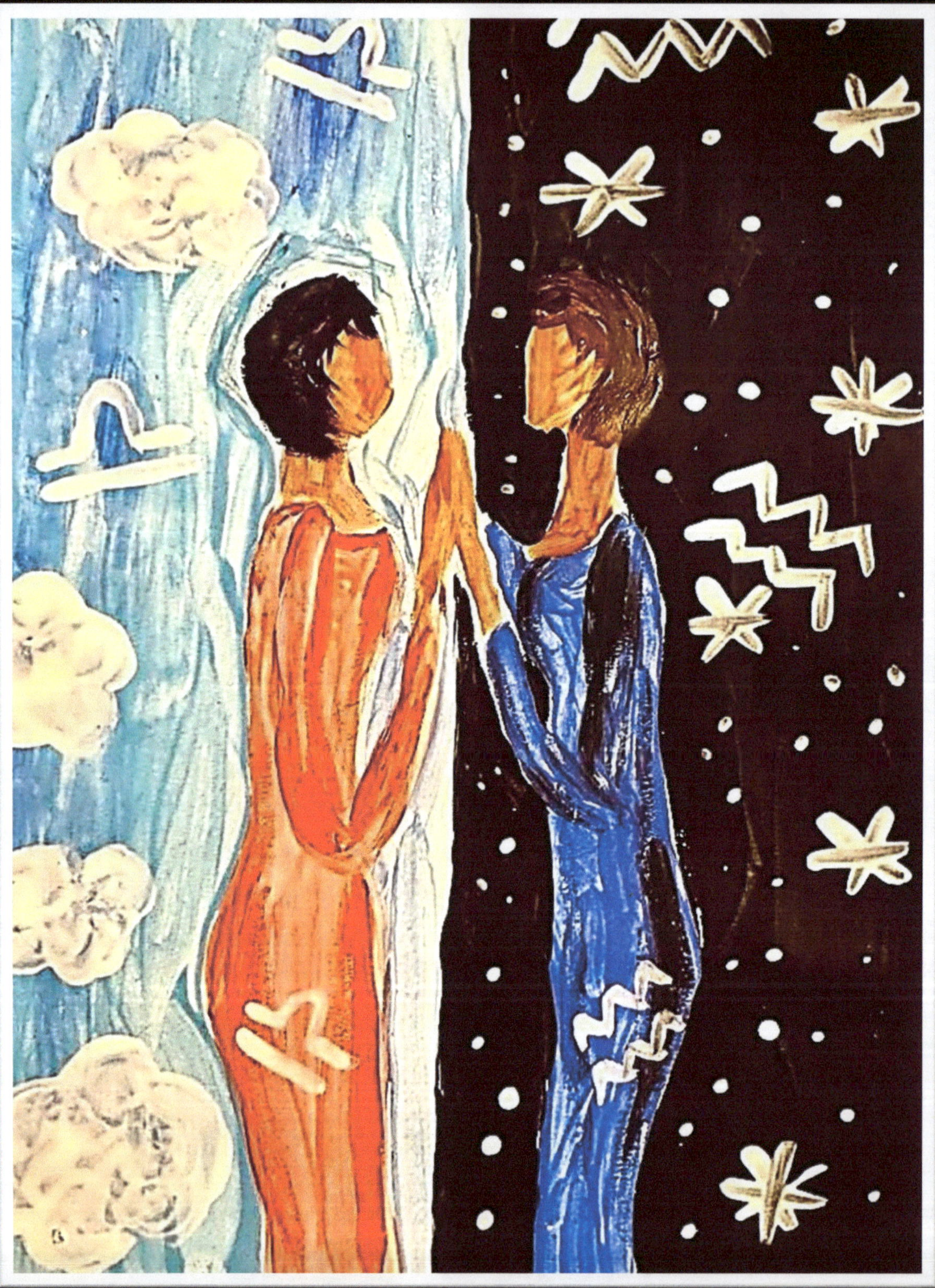

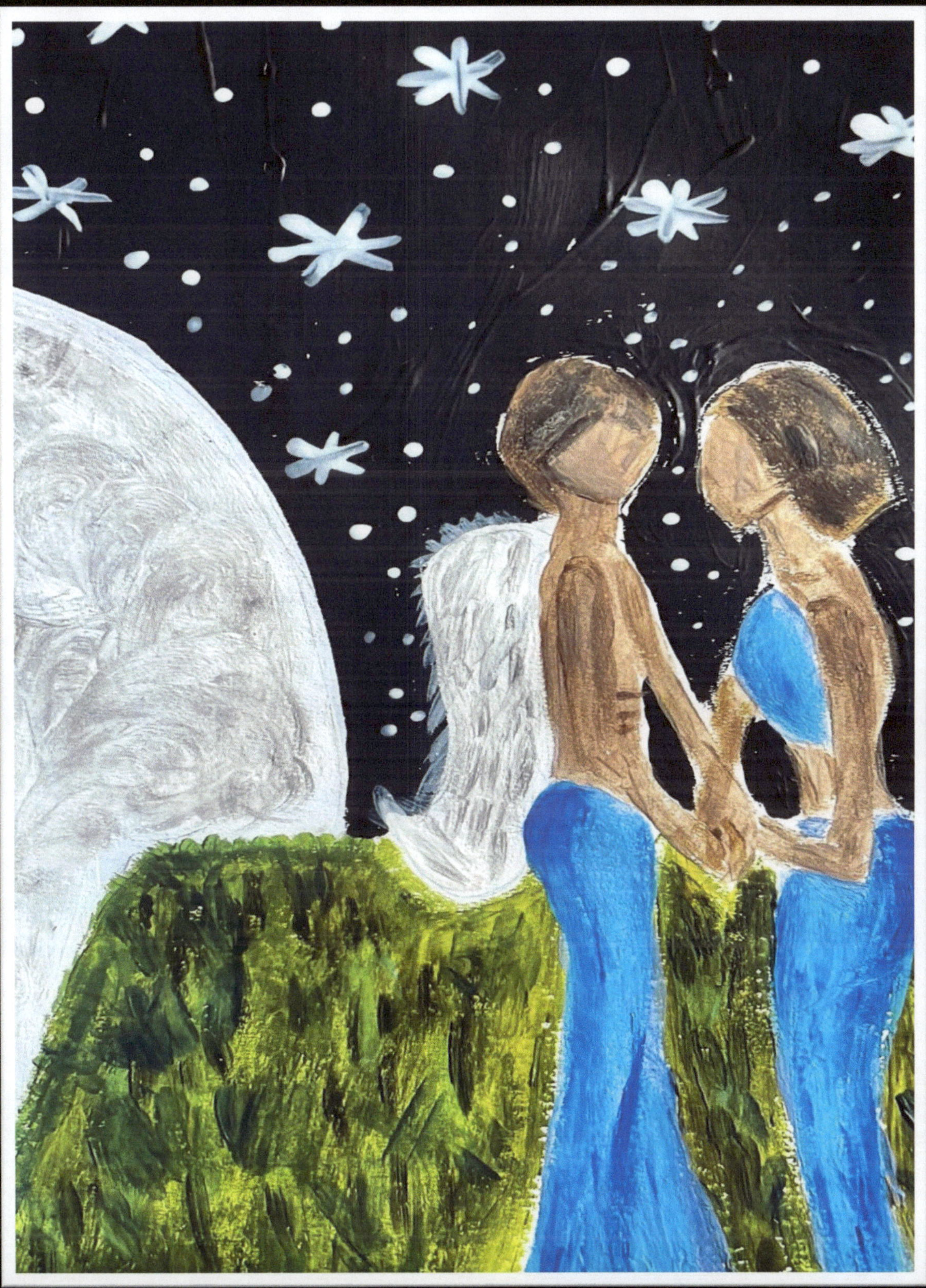

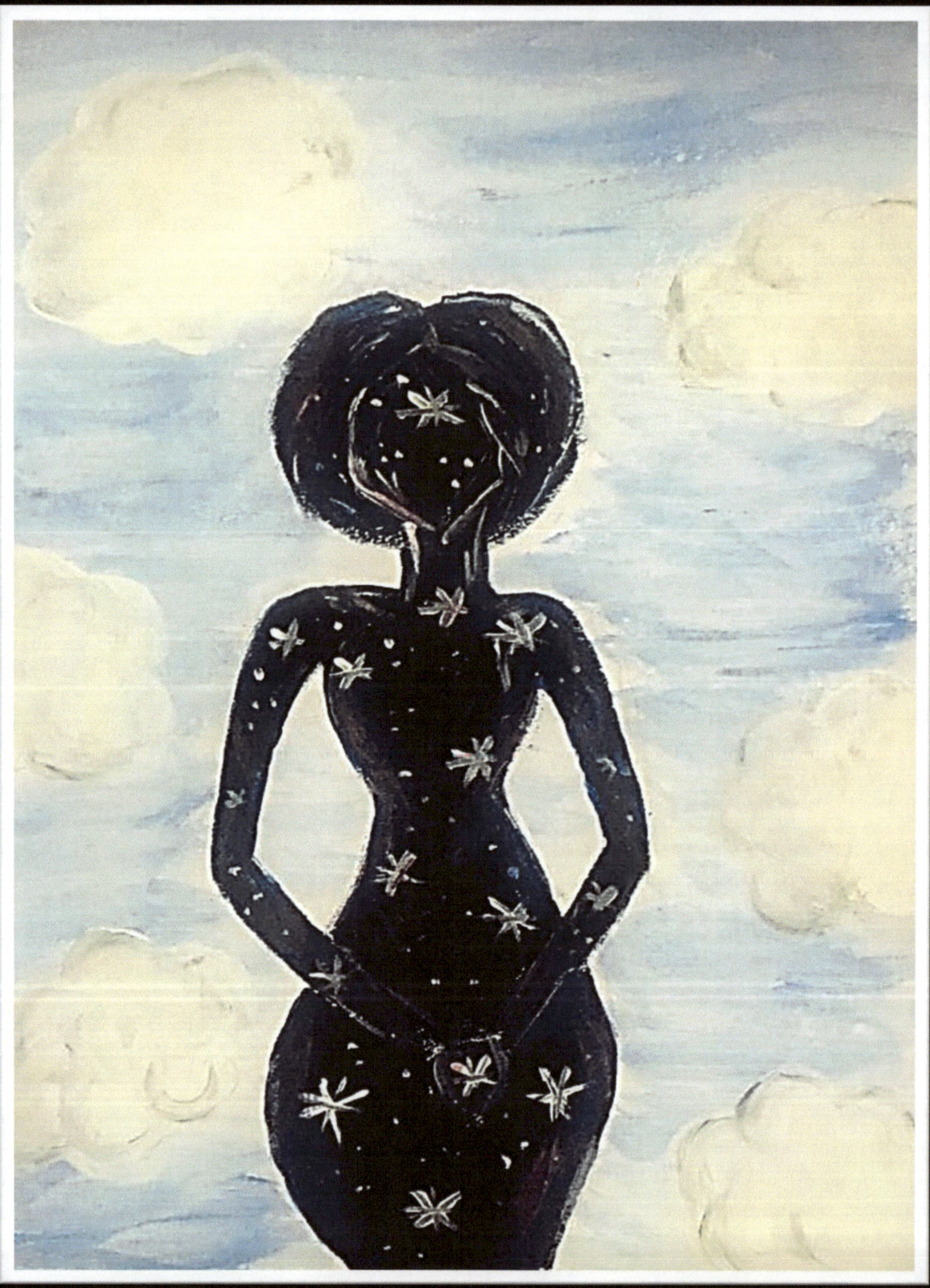

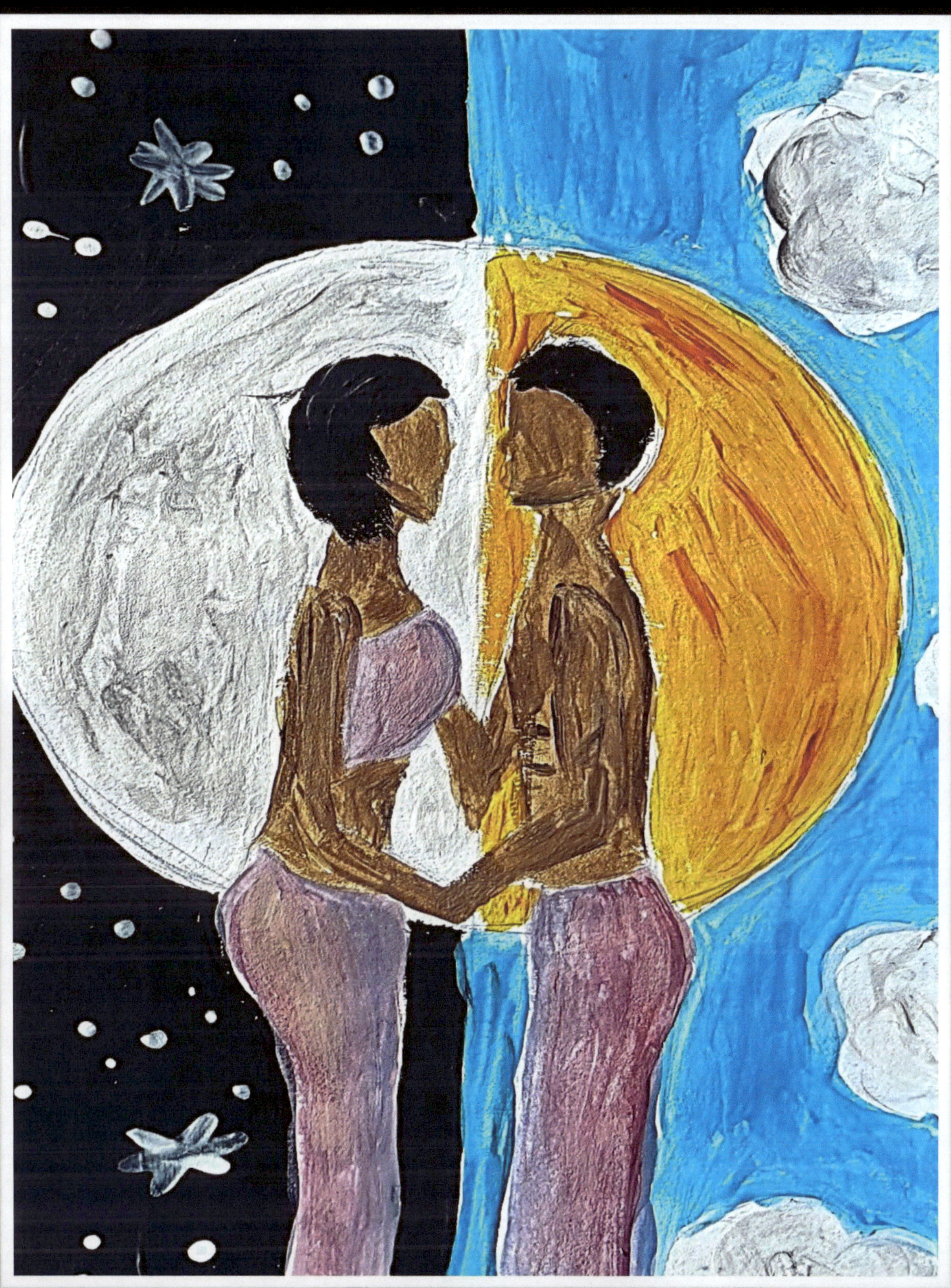

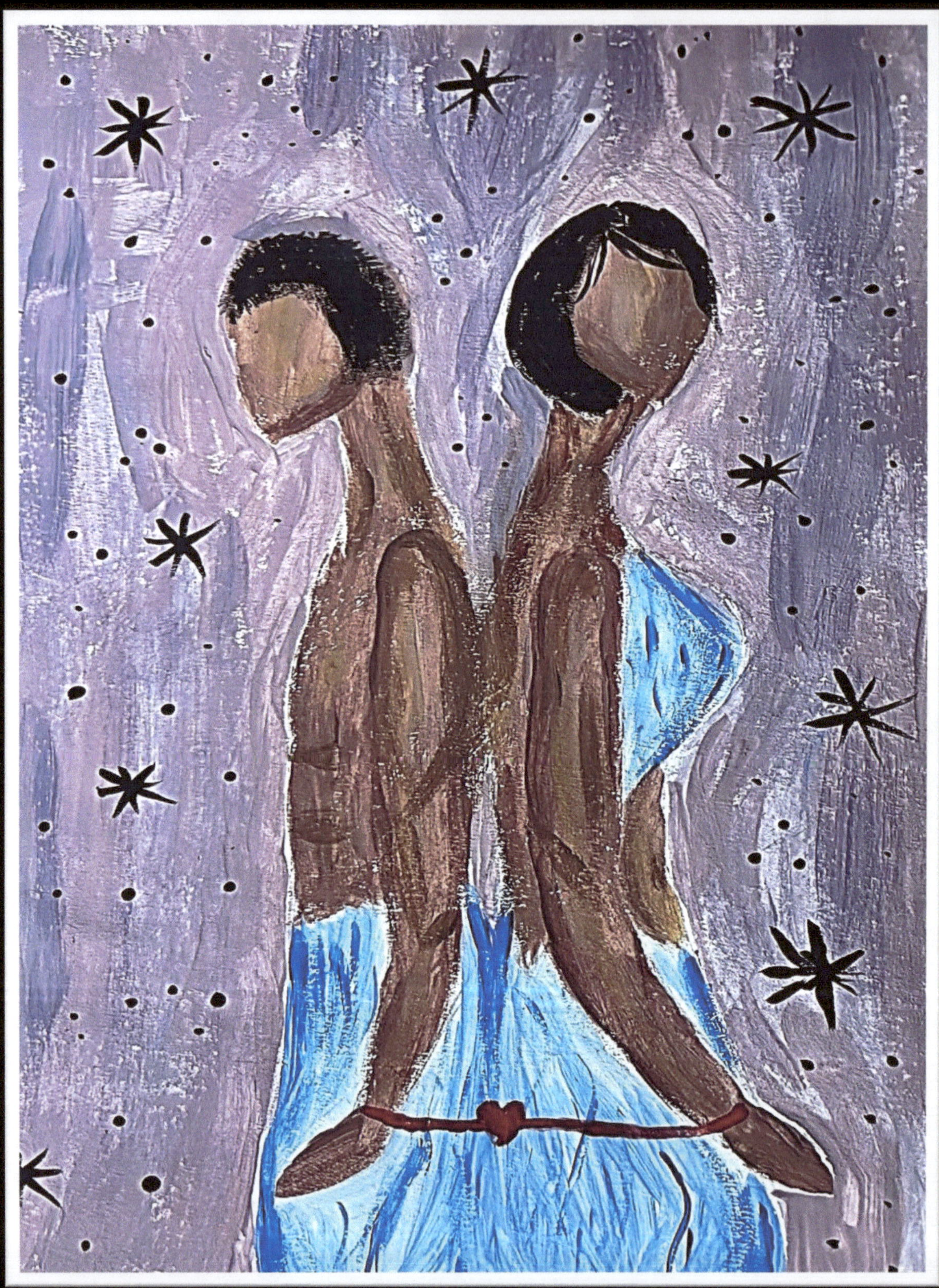

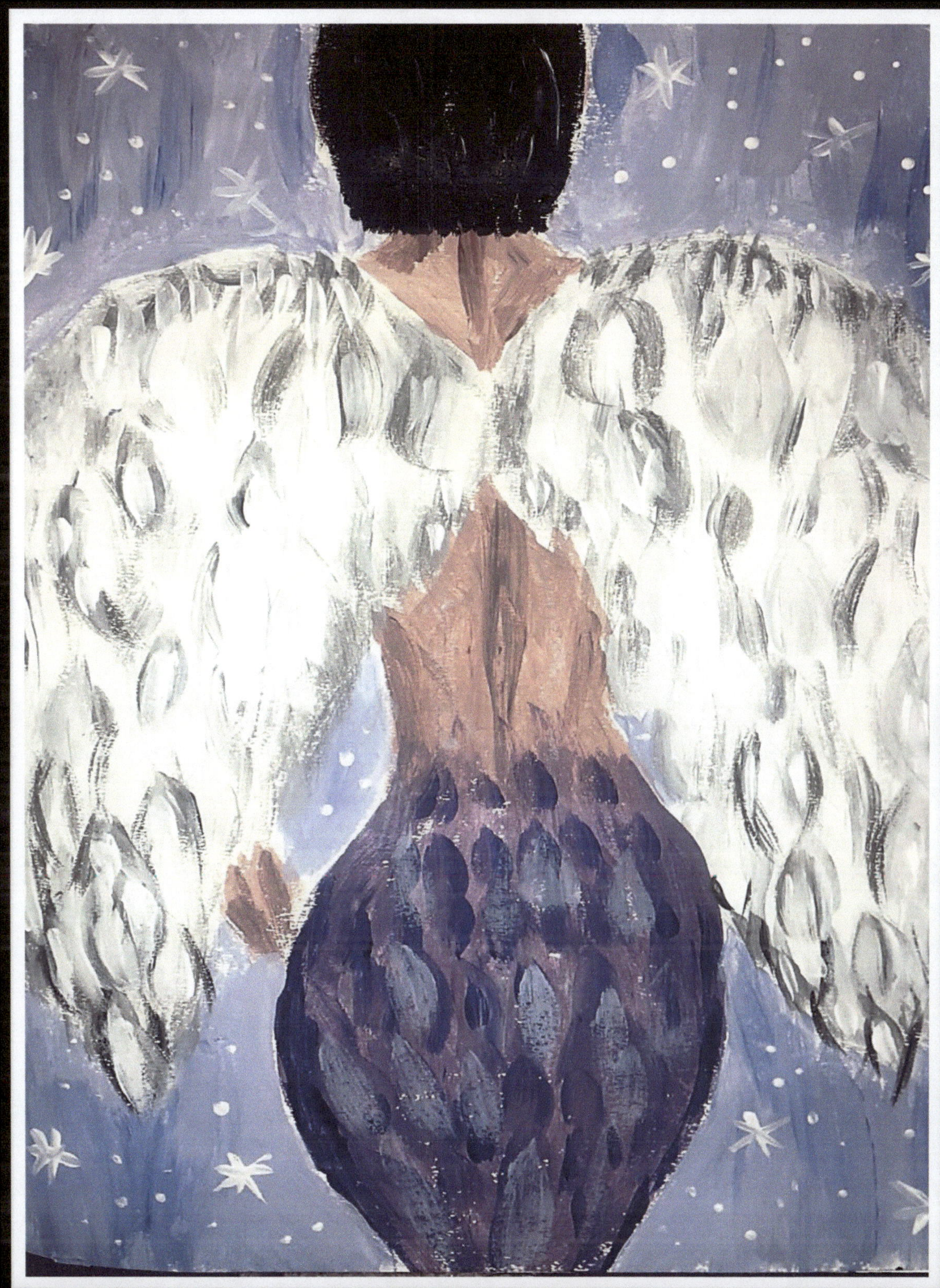

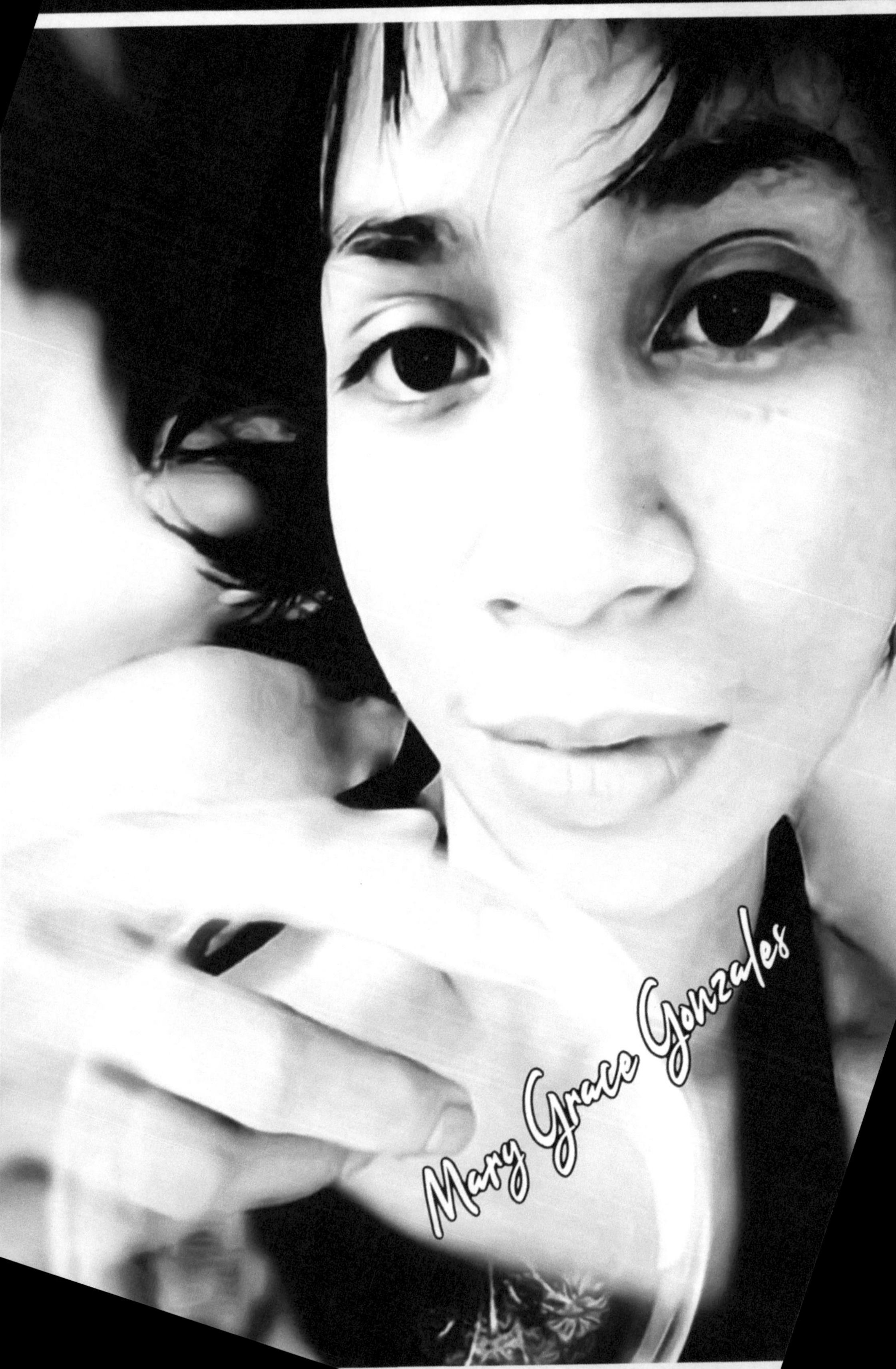
Mary Grace Gonzales

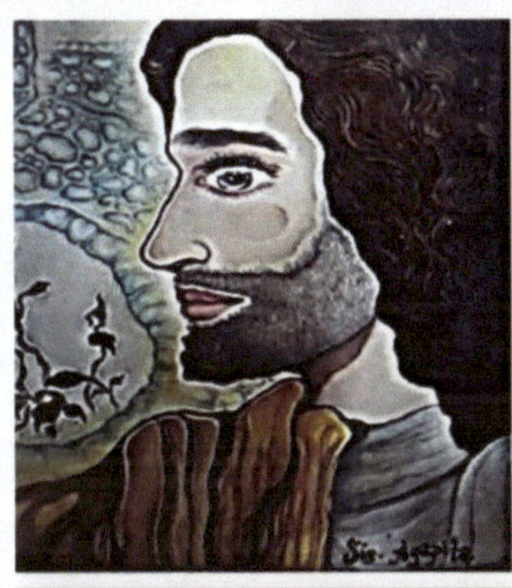
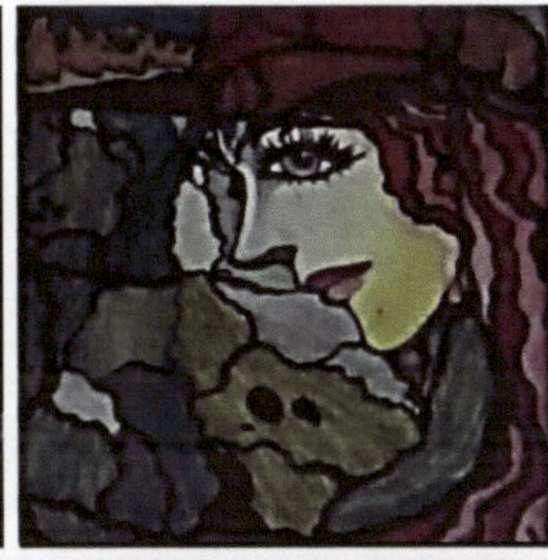
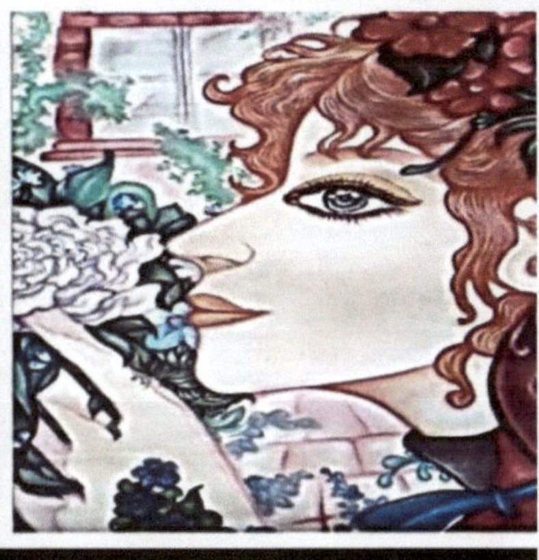

About Mary Grace Gonzales

MARY IS AN ARTIST, CARTOONIST AND POET FROM PILA, LAGUNA, PHILIPPINES. HER MOST RECENT ACHIEVEMENT WAS THE PUBLISHING OF HER POETRY BOOK "WHERE TO FIND ME."

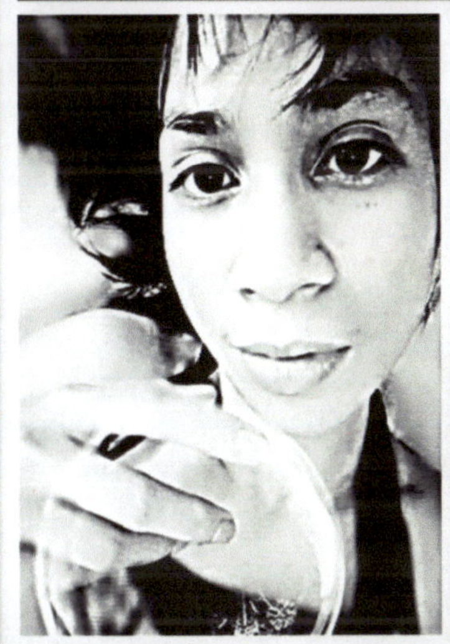
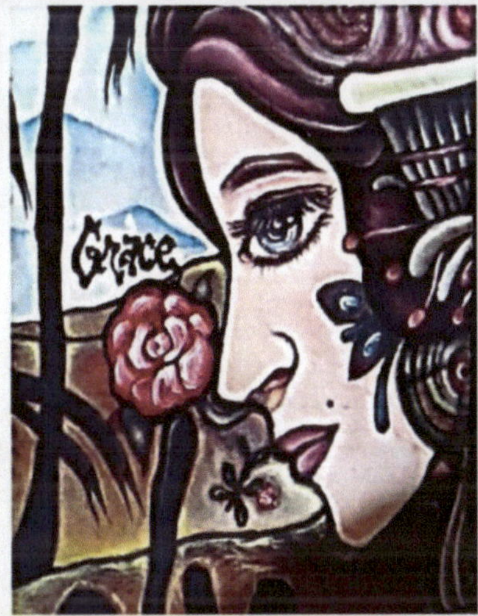

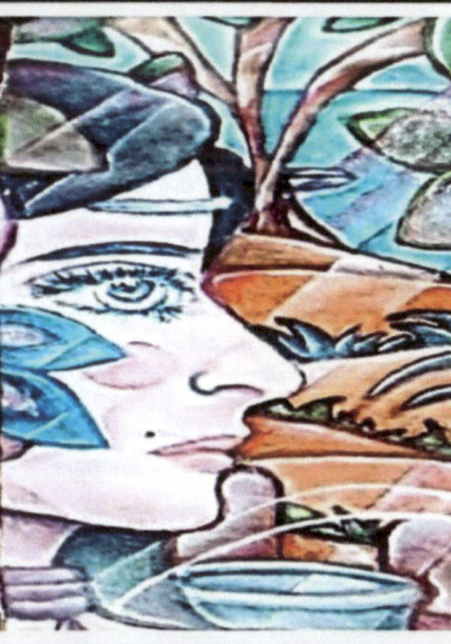

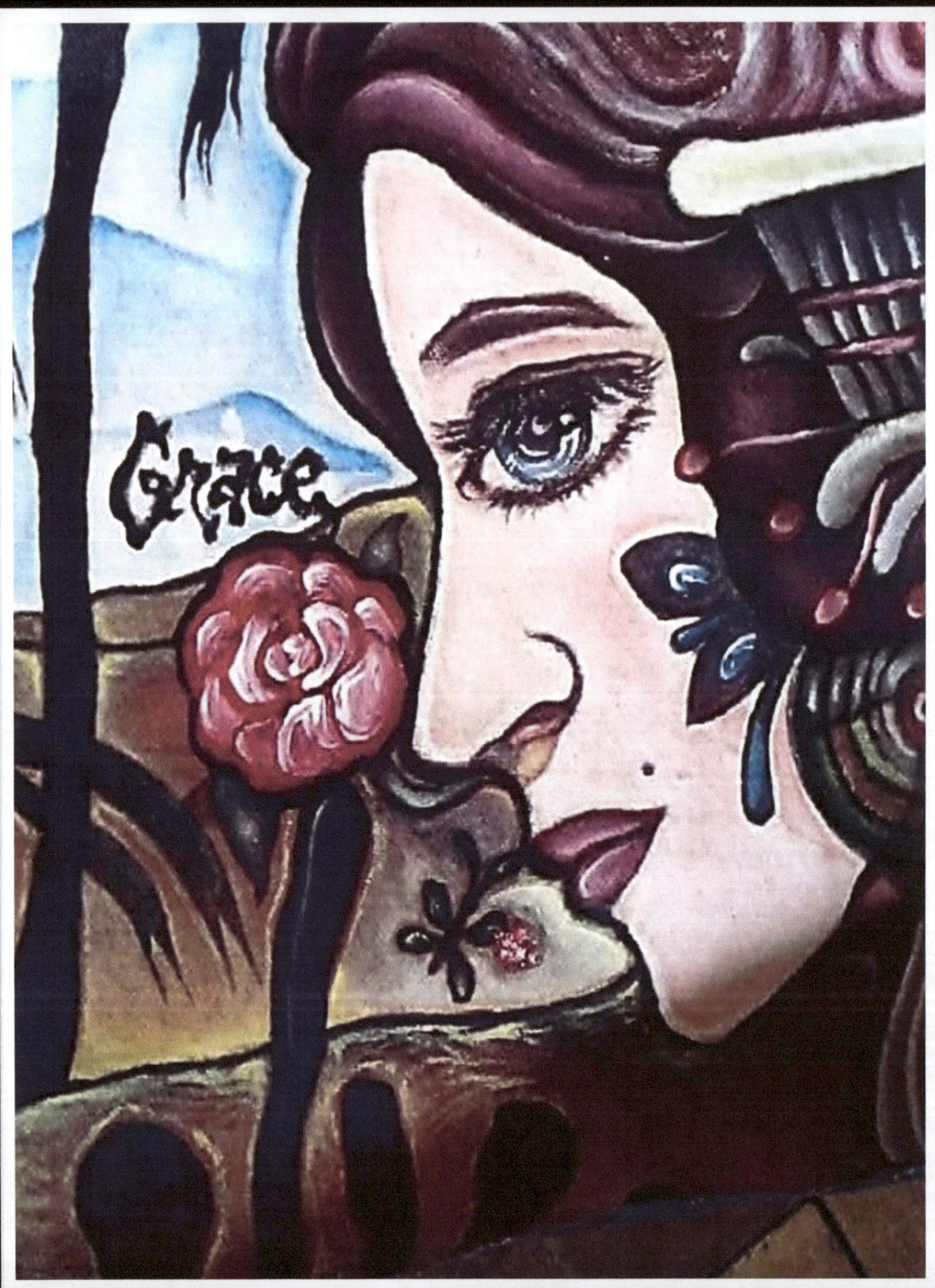
Grace

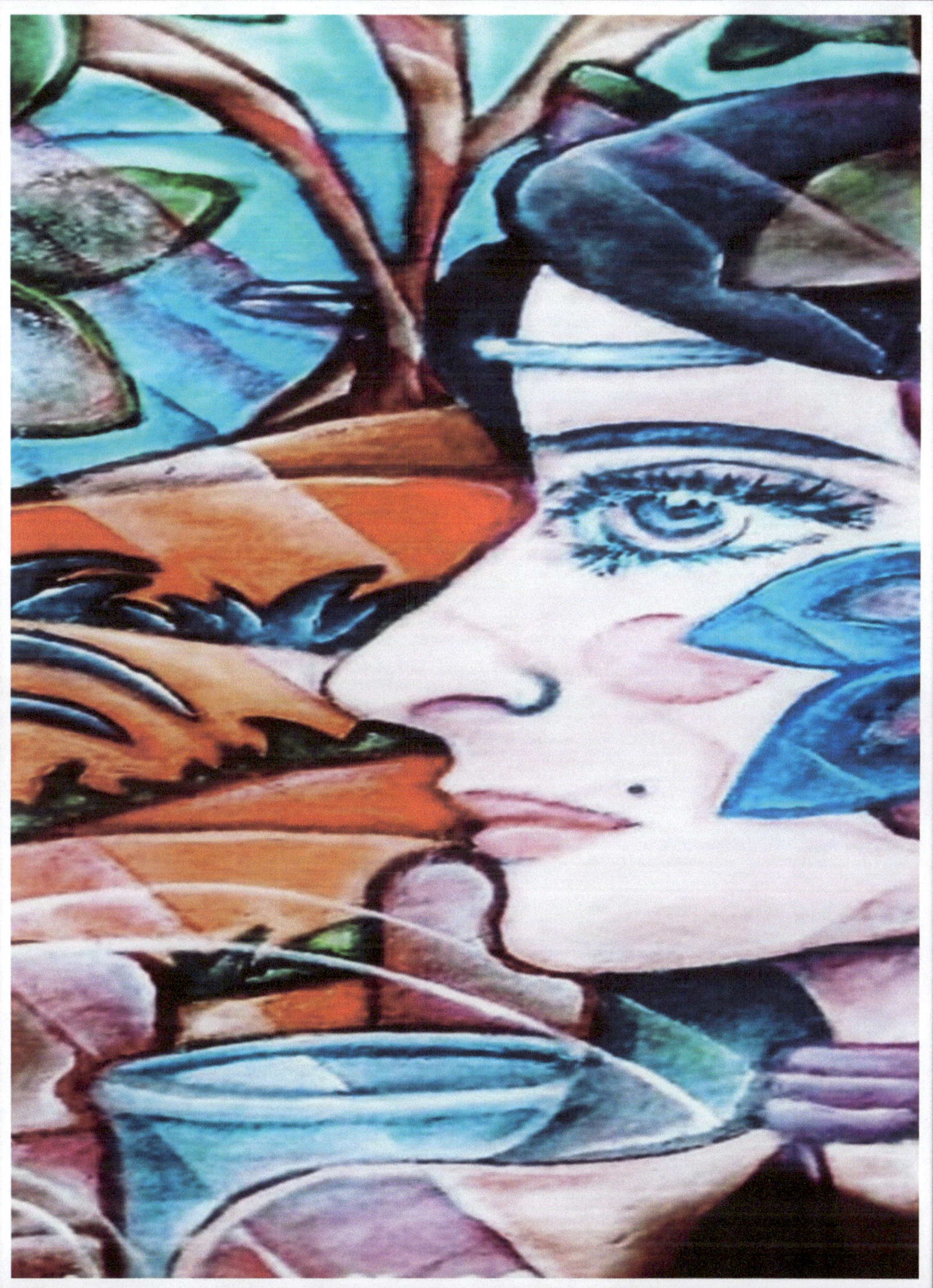

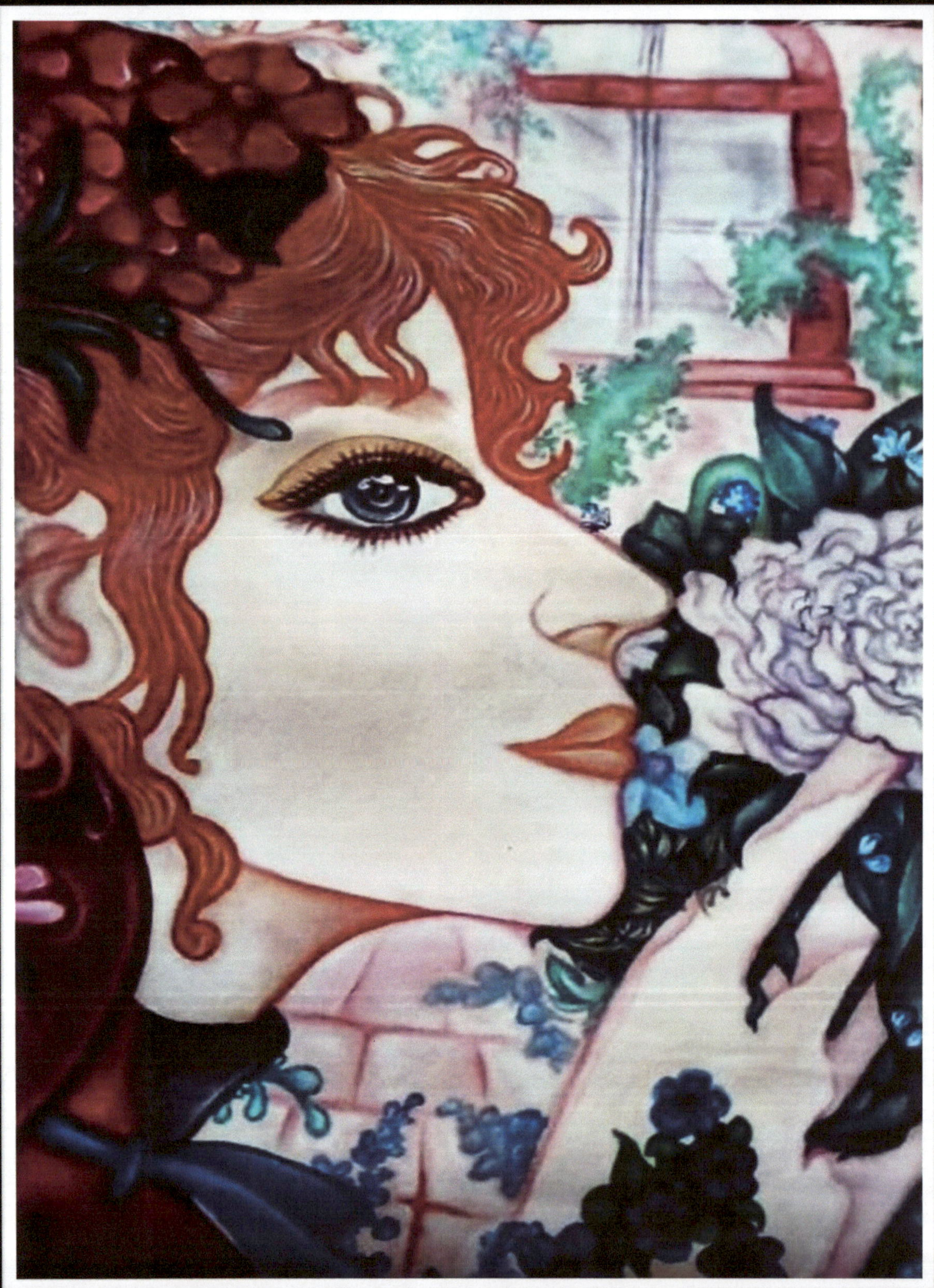

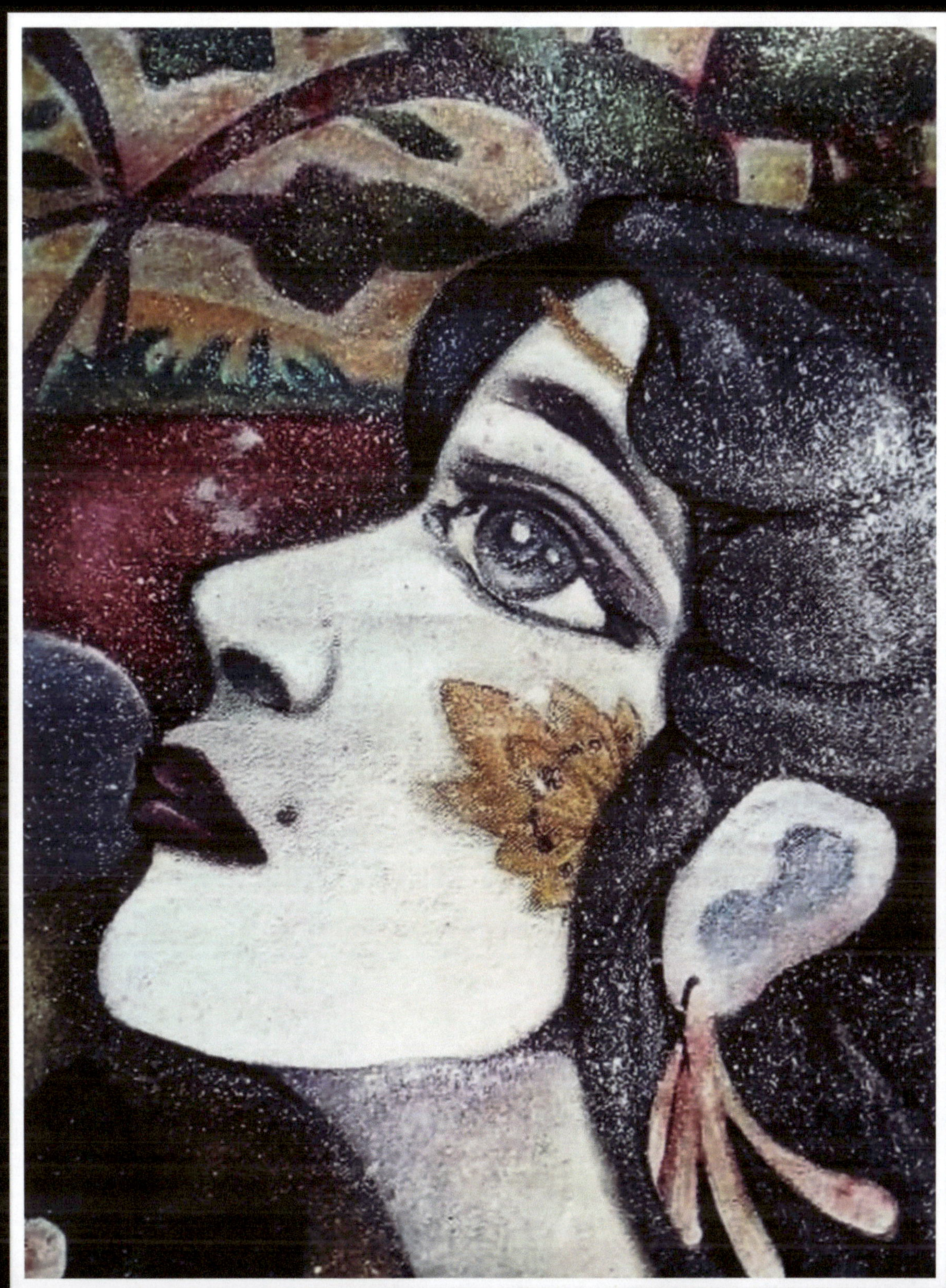

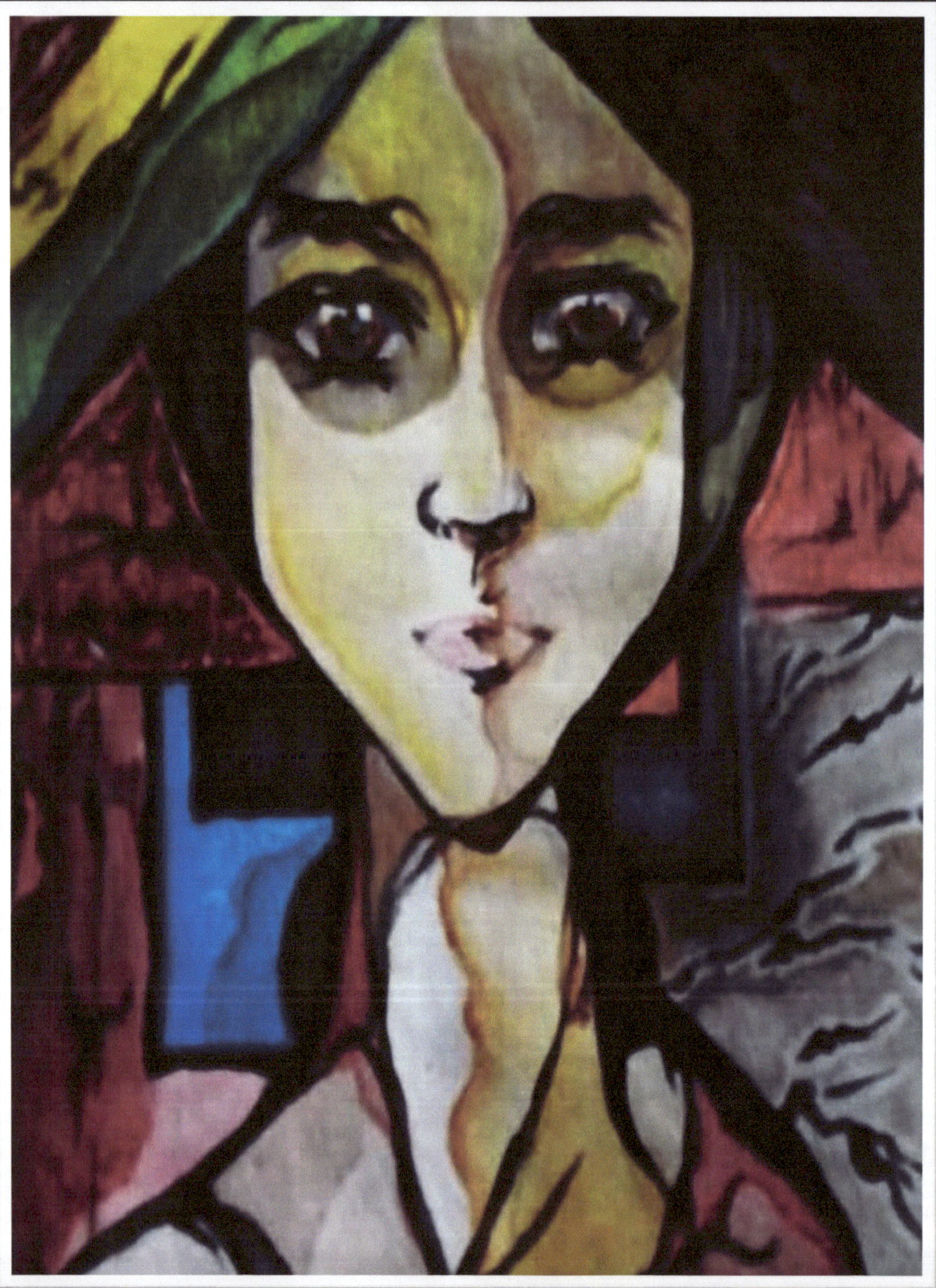

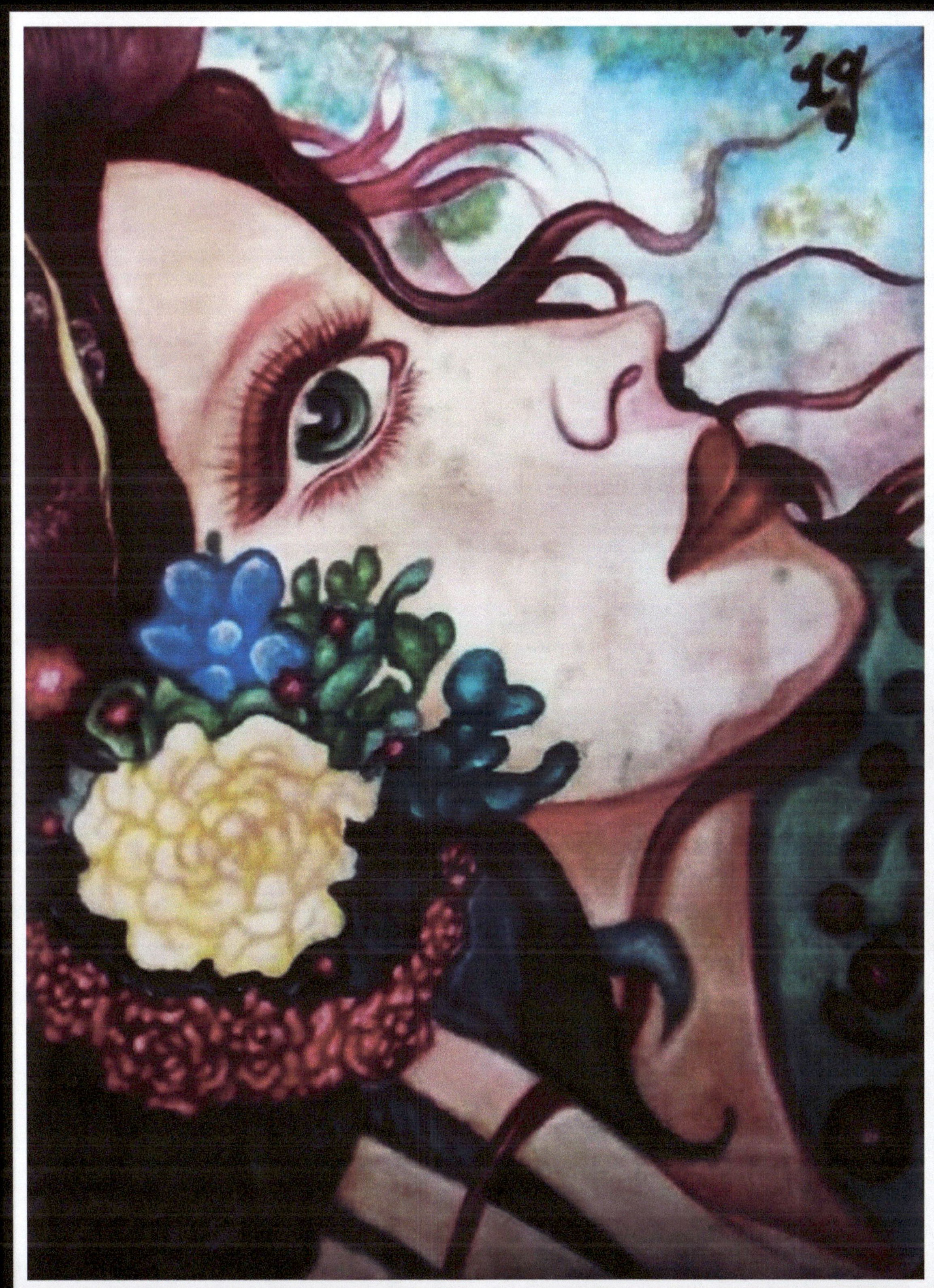

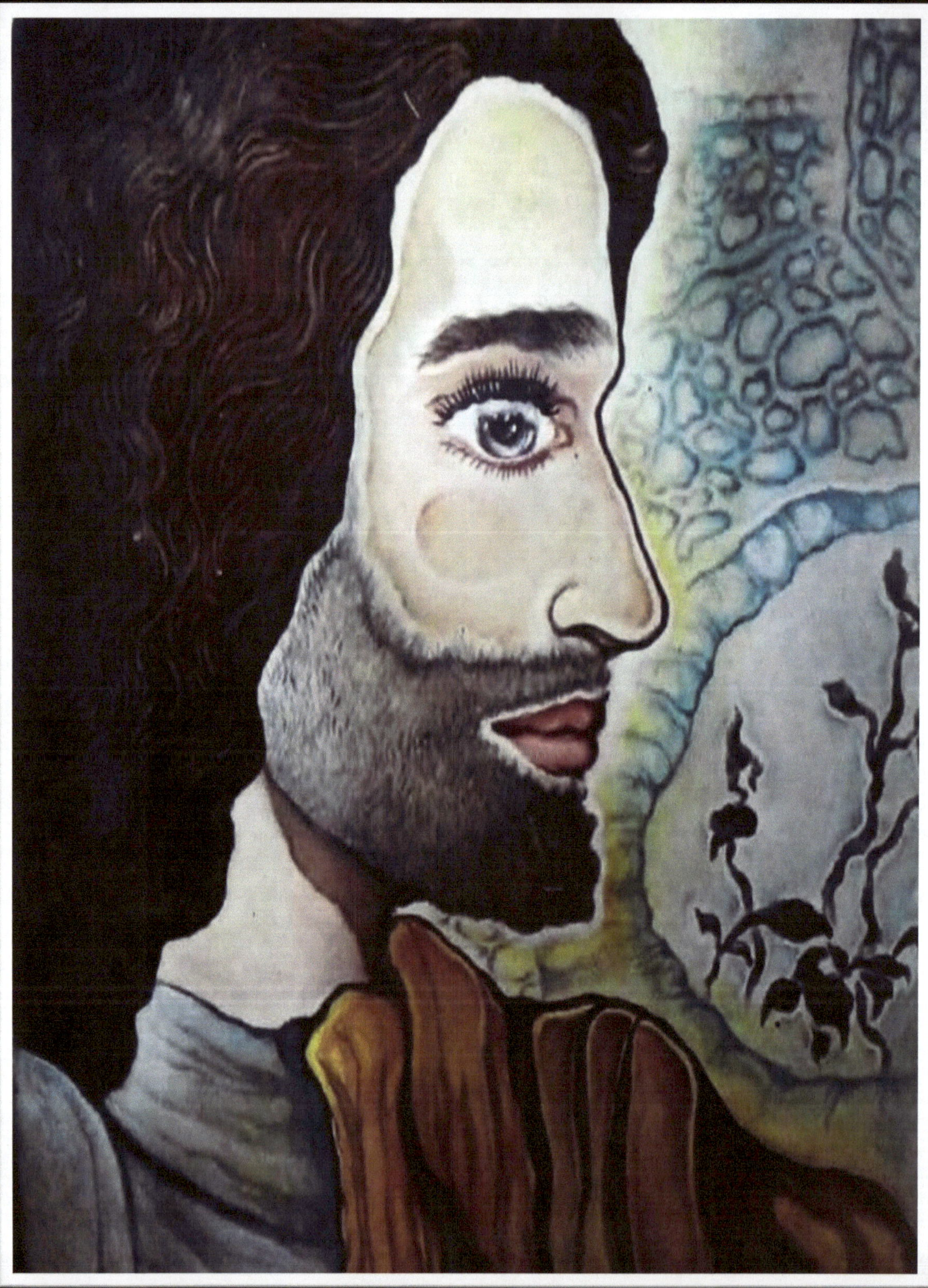

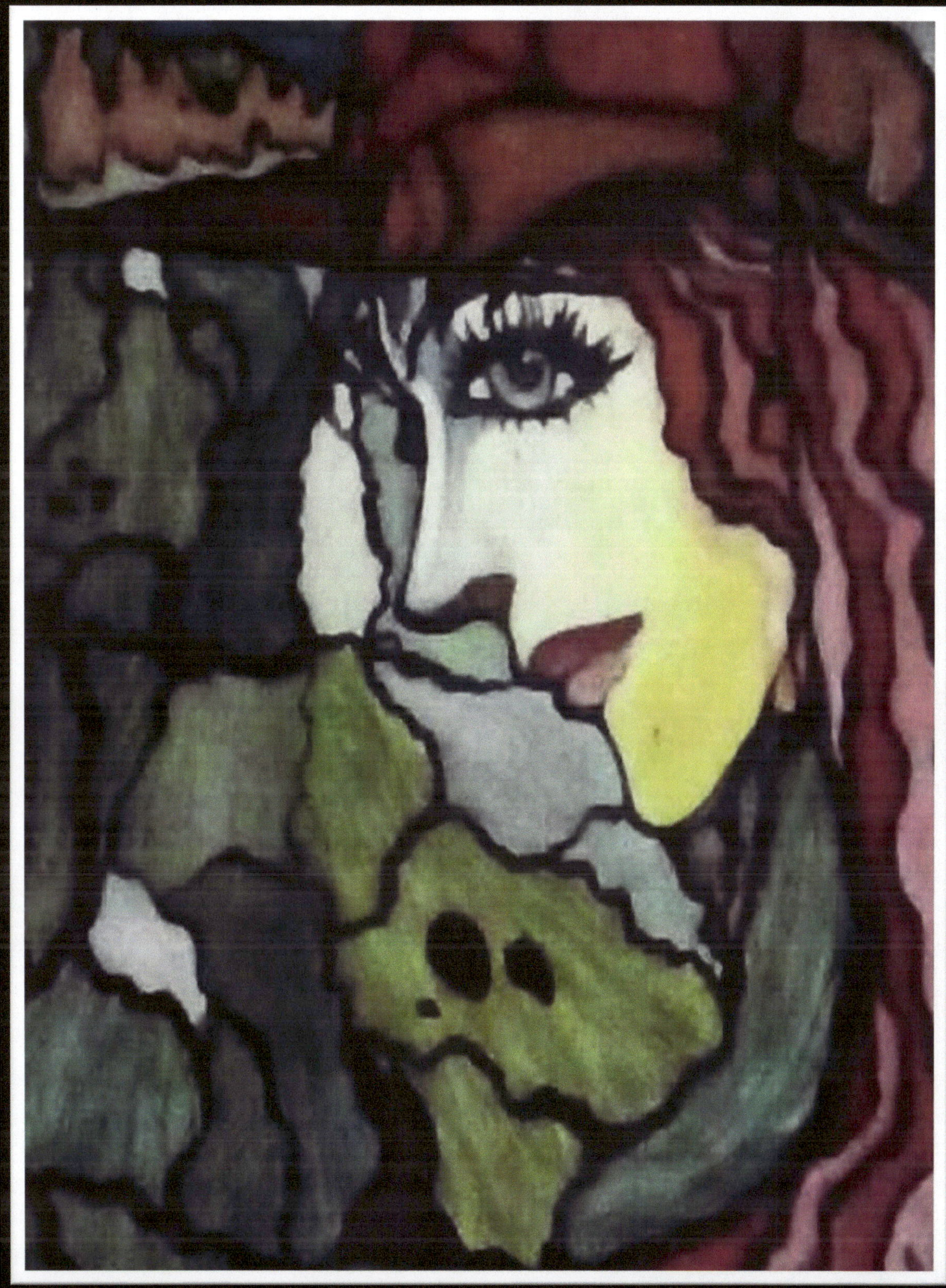

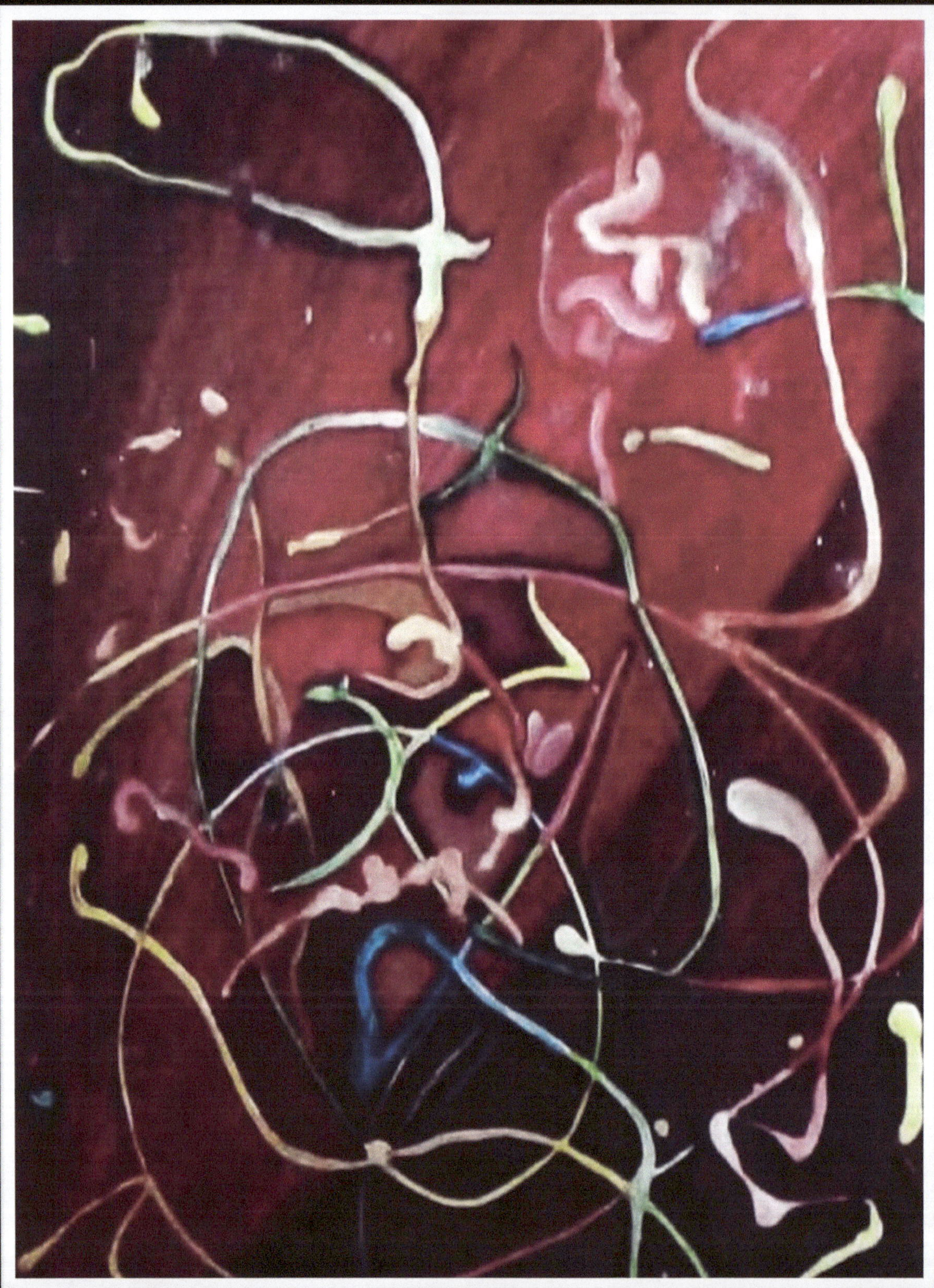

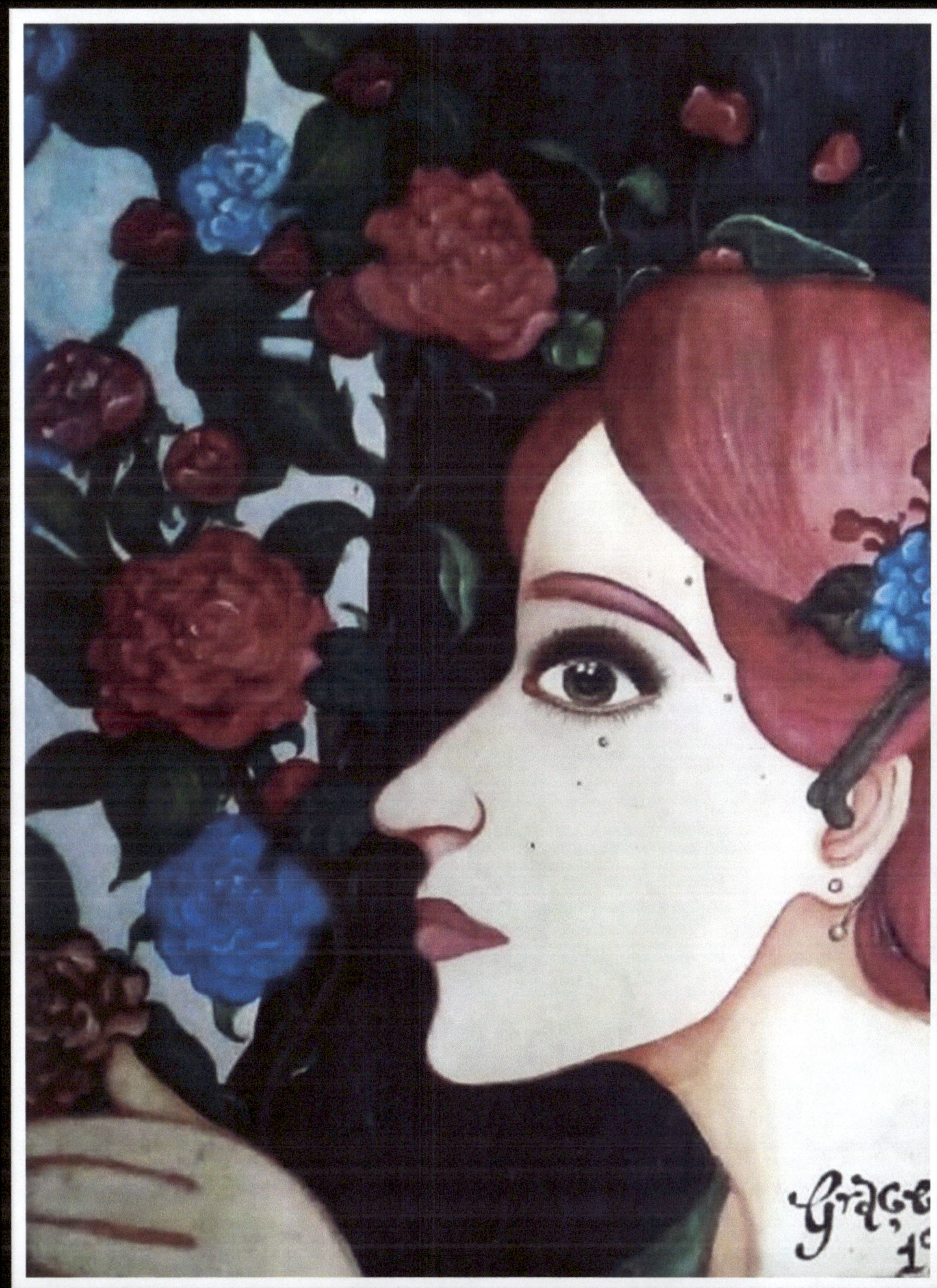

3 Amigos Ink and Splatter
The Lonely Soul in the Darkness
Volume 1 Issue 1
Edition 2

3 Amigos Ink and Splatter
The Lonely Soul in the Darkness
Volume 1
Issue 2

3 Amigos Ink and Splatter
The Lonely Soul in the Darkness
Volume 1
Issue 3

Check out...

3 Amigos Ink and Splatter
The Lonely Soul in the Darkness
Volume 1
Issue 4

3 Amigos Ink and Splatter:
The Lonely Soul in the Darkness
Volume 1, Issue 5
I Ain't Your Marionette

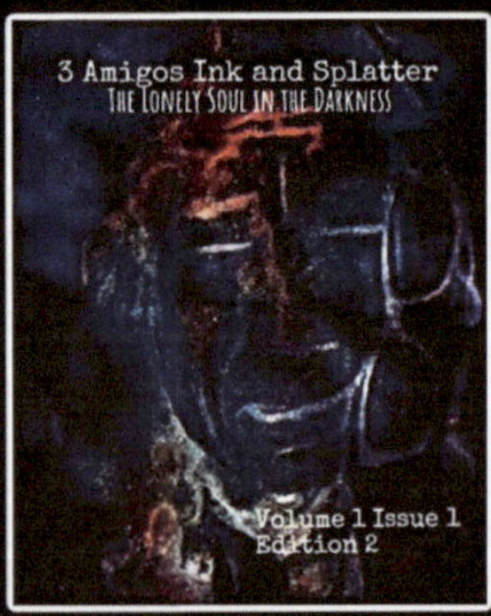

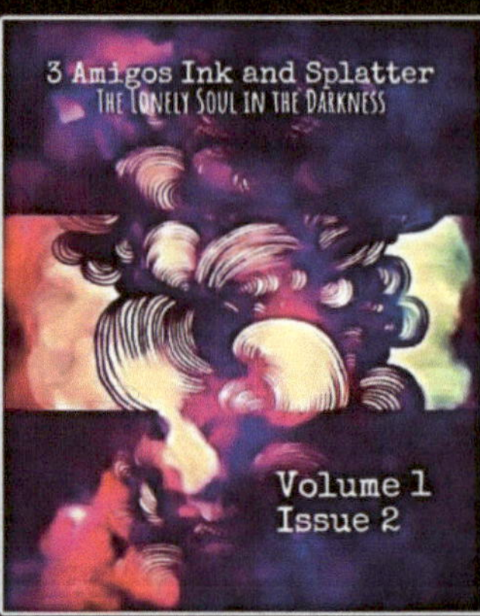

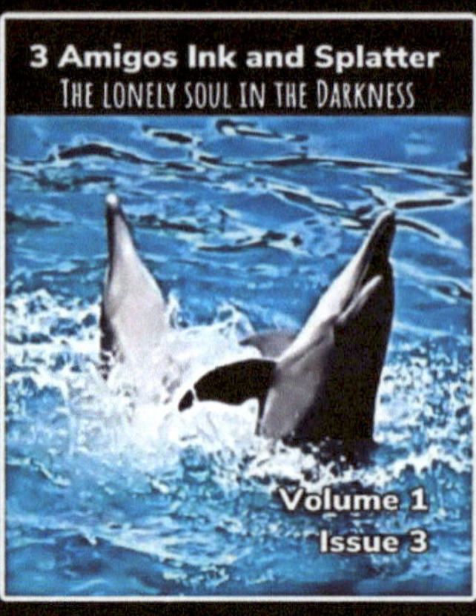

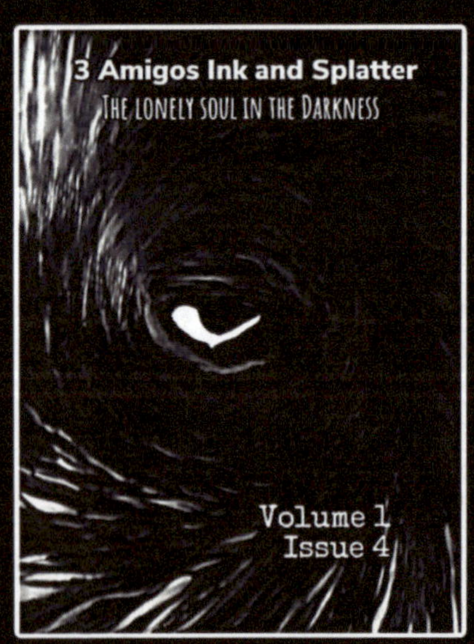

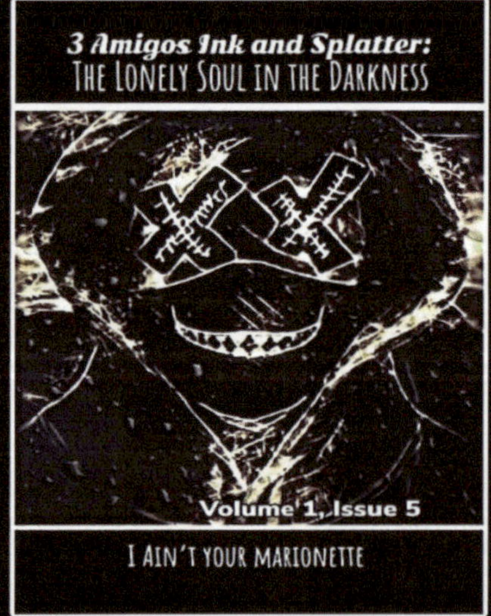

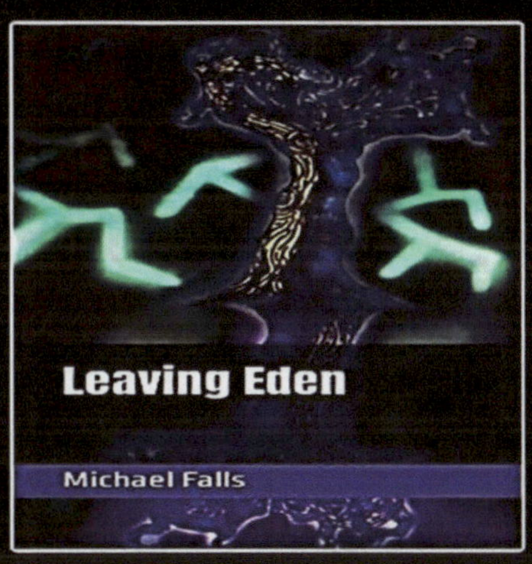
Leaving Eden
Michael Falls

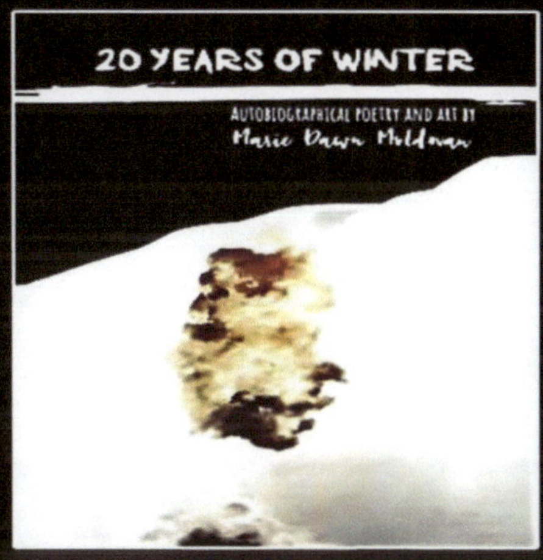
20 YEARS OF WINTER
AUTOBIOGRAPHICAL POETRY AND ART BY
Marie Dawn Moldovan

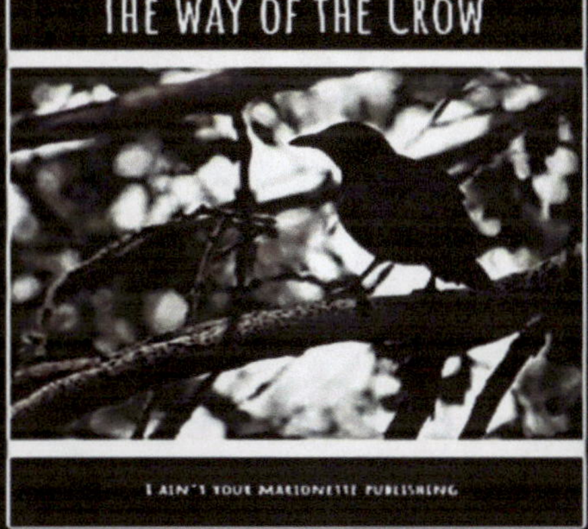
THE WAY OF THE CROW
I AIN'T YOUR MARIONETTE PUBLISHING

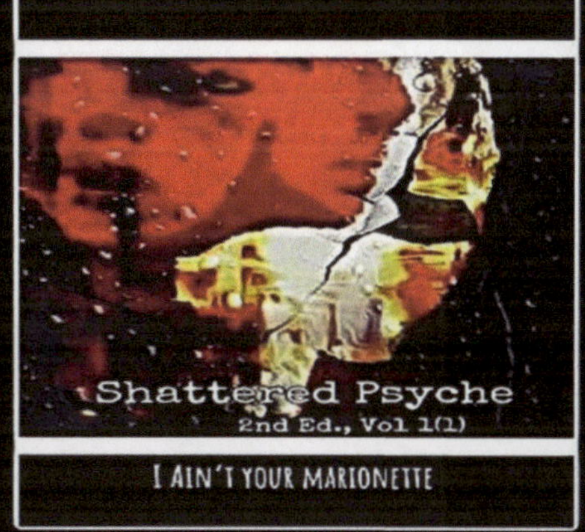
Shattered Psyche
2nd Ed., Vol 1(1)
I AIN'T YOUR MARIONETTE

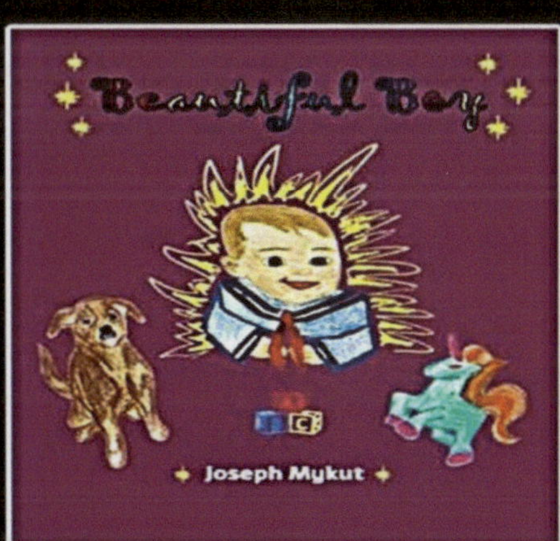
Beautiful Boy
Joseph Mykut

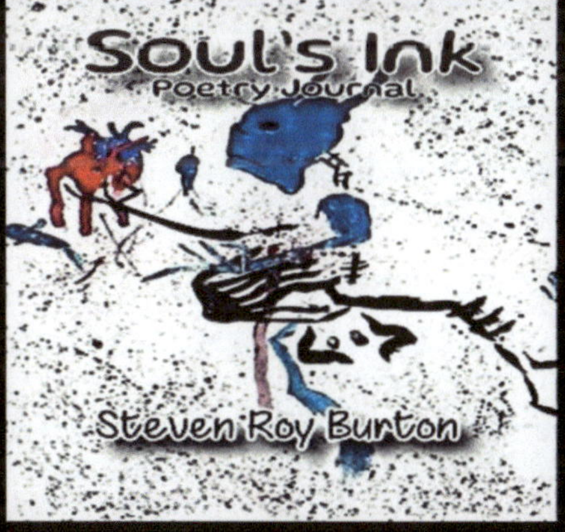
Soul's Ink
Poetry Journal
Steven Roy Burton

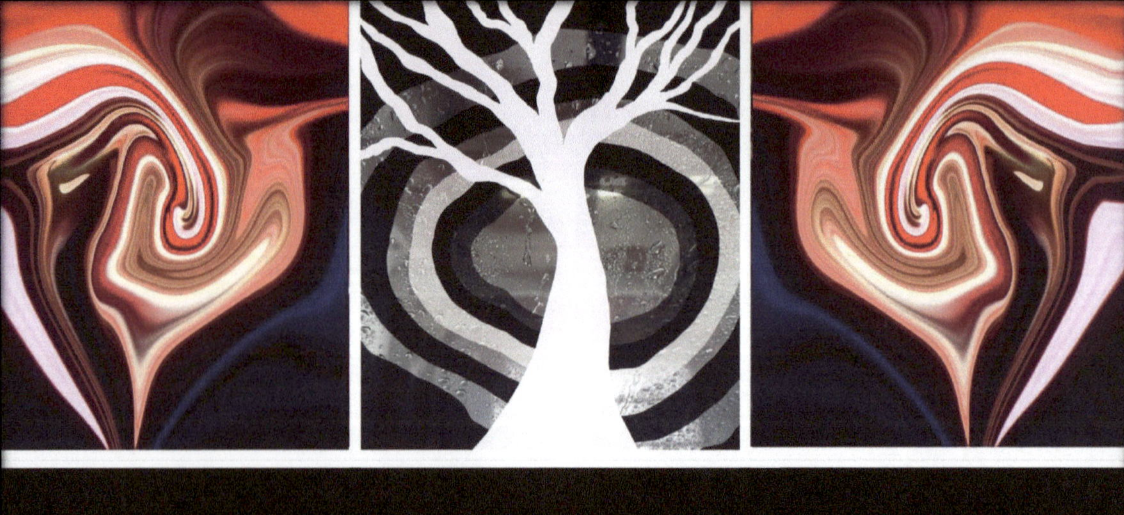

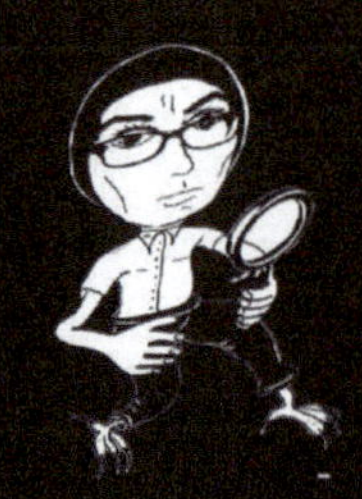

MAY EVERYDAY OF YOUR LIFE BE INKED WITH LOVE.

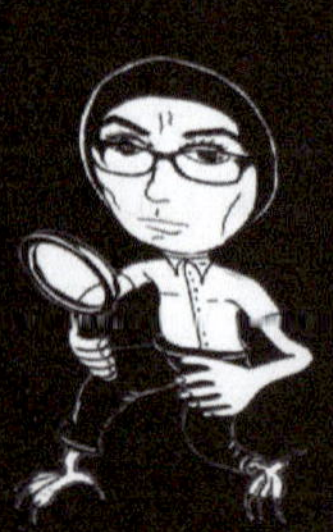

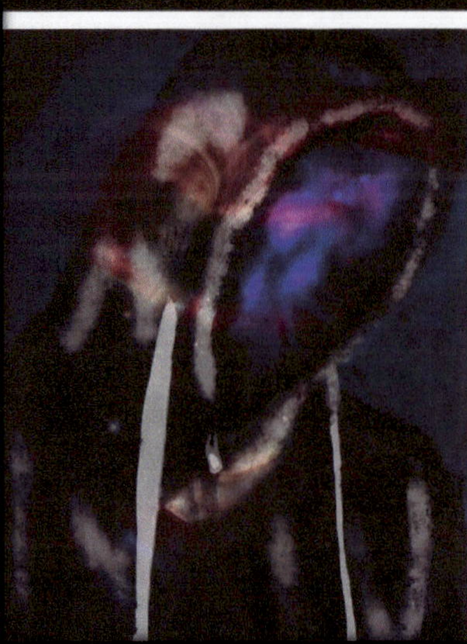

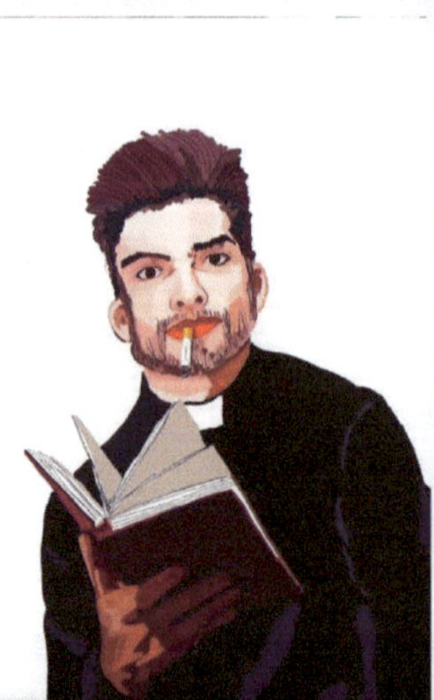

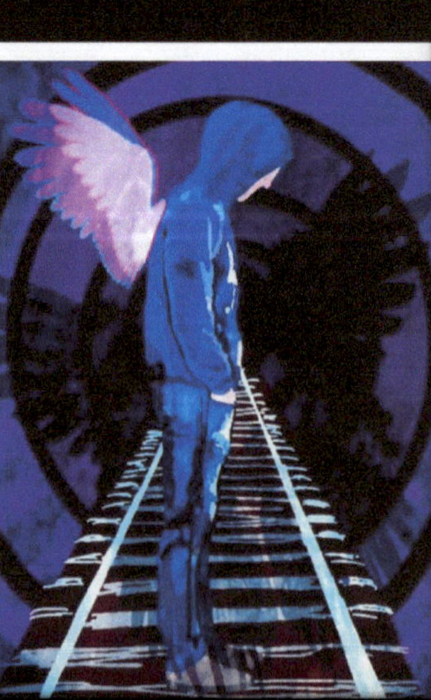

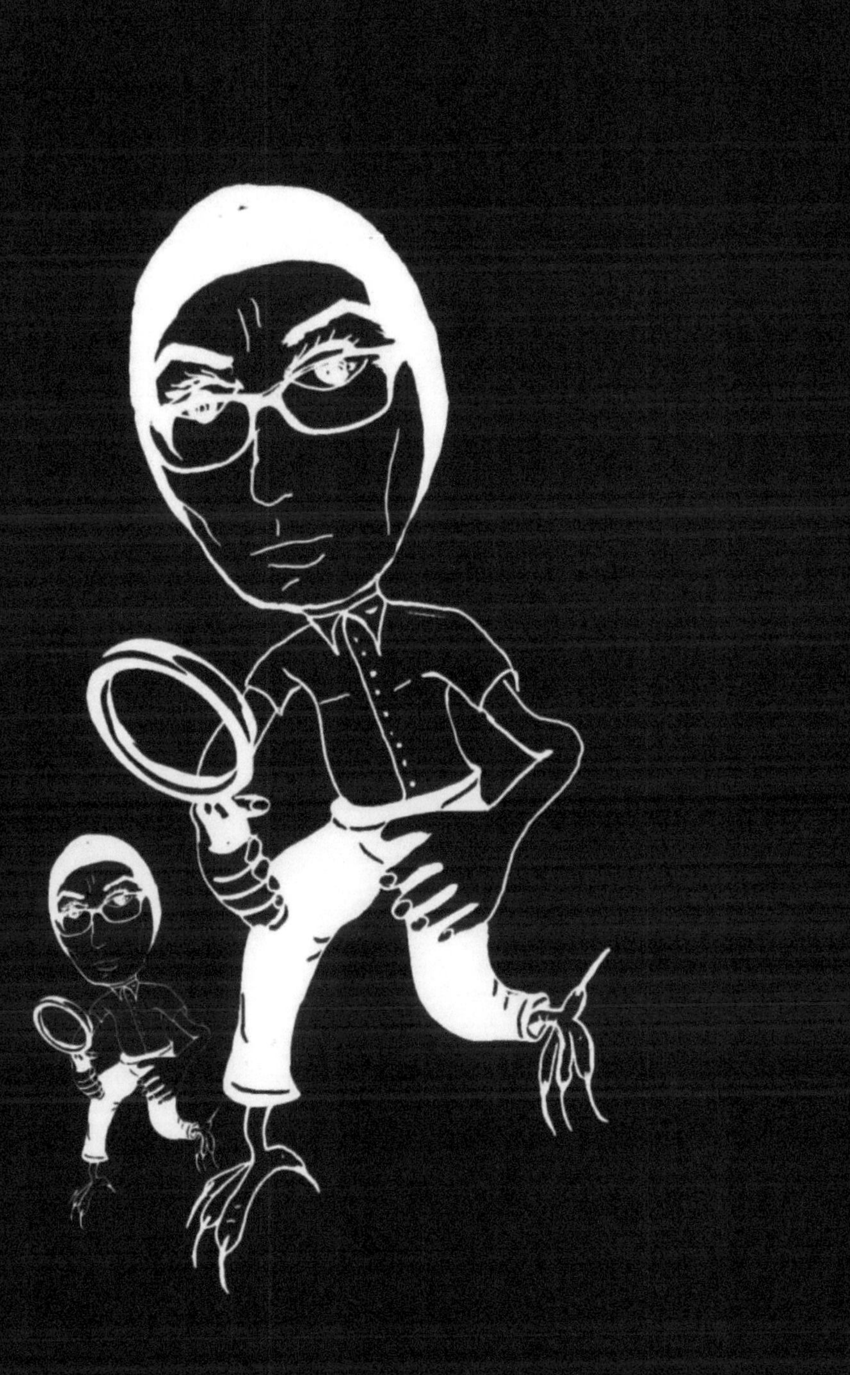

www.ingramcontent.com/pod-product-compliance
Lightning Source LLC
Chambersburg PA
CBHW042111030726
47599CB00002B/174